WRESTLING'S 101 STRANGEST MATCHES

OLIVER HURLEY

WRESTLING'S 101 STRANGEST MATCHES

OLIVER HURLEY

Pitch Publishing Ltd
A2 Yeoman Gate
Yeoman Way
Durrington BN13 3QZ

Email: info@pitchpublishing.co.uk
Web: www.pitchpublishing.co.uk

Published by Pitch Publishing 2010

A CIP catalogue record for this book is available from the British Library.

10-digit ISBN: 1905411766

13-digit ISBN: 9781905411764

Picture credits: Main cover image: courtesy of *Weekly Pro Wrestling*; filmstrip: courtesy of *Weekly Pro Wrestling*; Brian Berkowitz/Peter Lederberg collection; Howard Baum/hardwayart.com; Peter Lederberg; Phil Jones; andreakellaway.com; back cover: Ruth Oman/Peter Lederberg collection

andreakellaway.com pages 64, 77, 108
Howard Baum/hardwayart.com pages 16, 28, 62, 81
Brian Berkowitz/Peter Lederberg collection pages 38, 57, 70, 93
Courtesy of Chikara, Inc page 107
Courtesy of *Power Slam* page 35
Courtesy of Shockwave the Robot page 145
Courtesy of Jack Sinn page 116
Courtesy of *Weekly Pro Wrestling* pages 42, 86, 127, 132, 141, 157, 171
Oliver Hurley page 112
Bill Johnson page 162
Phil Jones pages 50, 67, 100, 158
Mike Lano pages 22, 47, 74, 130, 148, 176
Peter Lederberg pages 32, 82, 124
Bob Mulrenin page 172
Ruth Oman/Peter Lederberg collection pages 24, 137
Chris Swisher collection/csclassicwrphotos.com pages 44, 73
Scott Teal collection pages 55, 58, 123, 153

Design and illustration: Luke Jefford

Proof reader: Dean Rockett

Printed and bound in Great Britain by Cromwell Press Group

FOR
KATE

Oliver Hurley is a journalist and editor.
He has contributed to a wide variety of publications, including *The Big Issue*, *The Face*, *GamesMaster*, *The Guardian*, *Homes & Antiques*, *Metro* and *Power Slam*. He lives near Bristol.

CONTENTS

Foreword

When people find out that you're a professional wrestler, their first reaction is often a combination of astonishment and disbelief. And then when you tell them that you compete in the most violent and bloody matches the industry has to offer - so-called deathmatches - it's too much for most people to comprehend.

Apparently doing stunts into barbed wire, thumbtacks and fluorescent light tubes is not generally regarded as a fun way to spend your Saturday evenings. So what makes a man (or woman - as you'll read, these matches aren't solely the province of blokes) participate in such vicious fights?

I fell in love with wrestling when I was five years old. One of my earliest memories is watching a WWF match featuring 'El Matador' Tito Santana, while hiding under my mother's blanket on a stormy evening in the early 1990s. The flamboyant outfits of the superstars on television instantly fascinated me. My enthusiasm for the sport would only grow as time went on.

When I was a teenager, the wrestling business started to change drastically. Many of the glamorous, over-the-top characters disappeared and were replaced by personae based more on real life. Those were also the early years of the growth of the internet and it was this new medium that introduced me to Japanese hardcore wrestling. I remember my bewilderment and amazement when I found out what federations like Big Japan Pro Wrestling and Frontier Martial-Arts Wrestling brought to the table. Their combatants would throw each other into panes of glass, on to beds of nails and even into fire. Some of those wild brawls are portrayed in this book.

At the age of 15, a local wrestling promoter - knowing my enthusiasm for all things grappling - emailed me to ask if I was interested in training at his school in Nuremberg, Germany, 105 miles away from my hometown of Munich.

Back then, I did not have any ambitions of becoming a professional wrestler but when you are young you pretty much give everything a shot, especially when it promises danger. I soon realised that I had a decent amount of talent when it came to performing flips and trading holds, so I stuck with it. I also discovered my rather high pain threshold, a useful attribute in this industry. On 4 August 2001 - just two weeks after my sixteenth birthday - I debuted in the squared circle.

It did not take me long to notice that the European wrestling scene was missing something back then. Only a handful of guys - notably my good friend Peter 'Hate' Wiechers and a Dutchman who called himself Mad Cow - were including hardcore elements in their fights. Even then, their use of weapons was unspectacular compared to the craziness in Japan and several independent promotions in the United States. But that level of innovation and brutality was something I would have loved to have seen in Europe as a fan. Since nobody else was going that far, I decided to step up. If I wasn't going to do it, nobody else was. Still being underage did not hinder me from competing in some of the most violent and gory matches Europe had ever seen.

The inevitable consequence was countless injuries. I completely tore the ACL in my left knee, the PCL in my right knee, broke my collarbone, suffered concussions, endured snapping hip syndrome, lost parts of my teeth, broke my nose several times and collected scars like other people collect stamps. The main motivation for putting my body through all this was always to do things that nobody else had ever done before and entertain people at the same time. I pride myself with the innovative match types I came up with and competed in.

In particular, the infamous *Saw* deathmatch between me and the Indianapolis-based Drake Younger - in which we used weapons inspired by the *Saw* horror movie franchise - became an underground favourite. A chair with dozens of razor blades sticking out of its seat cushion, a saw and a power drill were all used in this surreal match. It took place in a rundown warehouse in Krefeld, Germany in front of 35 fans, all of whom were on a guest list in order to avoid any legal problems.

Another unique concept was the boiler room ladder match I had against my fellow countryman Steve Douglas. At the time, I was playing a character loosely inspired by Gollum from *The Lord of the Rings*, who resided in a boiler room - which is where the match began. From there, we would brawl into the arena, where the goal was to climb a ladder and retrieve the title belt that we were fighting for from the ceiling. Such a match had never been done before and has never been done since. Curiously enough, the boiler room part was taped in Dortmund a month before the ladder match, which took place in Oberhausen. Why? The venue in Oberhausen didn't have a boiler room.

You see, I have had my share of strange matches. But one of the strangest - and the one featured later on in the book - was my first round match in Combat Zone Wrestling's *Tournament of Death*. My ultimate goal as a deathmatch wrestler was always to compete in this world-renowned tournament.

When my chance finally came in June 2009, I focused on leaving a lasting impression. My opponent, DJ Hyde, collected me from Philadelphia International Airport the evening before the big show. We were on our way to pick up his girlfriend while we discussed how to hurt each other in the most creative way. I had come up with the idea of using cinder blocks. Brilliant. Even more brilliant was my plan to build a structure composed of a couple of those blocks elevating a pane of glass. I was then going to pour lighter fluid on the glass and set it on fire. Stupid me would, of course, be the victim of this evil construction.

'DJ, do you think the fire is gonna go out as soon as I break the glass?' I asked. 'I mean, technically, as soon as the glass is broken, there's nothing left to burn, right?'

'Yeah, I think you're right!'

It turned out that the both of us had apparently never paid attention in physics classes. Or chemistry. Or wherever it is that they tell you not to set glass on fire and let people throw you through it from the top rope of a wrestling ring without you even wearing a shirt for protection.

When my exposed back broke the glass, the fire did not go out. Instead, a huge fireball rose into the air. I instantly realised that my hair and my shoulder had caught fire. Panicking, I rolled around like a madman and tried to get out of the ring as quickly as possible. One of the cinder blocks was lying right underneath the bottom rope and cost me a valuable second. A second is a long time when you are on fire.

The following moments seemed to last an eternity. I was squirming in pain on the outside of the ring, waiting for the ring crew to extinguish the fire. They finally managed to get it under control. DJ Hyde covered me and I... kicked out. I should have just called it a day. After all, I had just suffered third-degree burns. But this was just the beginning of a long and painful day featuring two more brutal rounds.

I'll say this much: a minute before we got to his girlfriend's place the night before the show, DJ Hyde stressed *one* thing in particular. 'TJ, please don't tell her what we've got planned for the finish!'

Alexander Bedranowsky AKA Thumbtack Jack
myspace.com/thumbtackjack

Introduction

Professional wrestling is, by its very nature, strange – a violent ballet that defies both fashion and logic. Even a standard match consists of two men going through the motions of engaging in a choreographed brawl with one another, generally using moves that could never work in a real fight, while wearing skin-tight costumes predominantly composed of luridly-coloured spandex. However you try to explain it – and even quoting the 1957 essay on wrestling by semiologist Roland Barthes won't get you out of this one – wrestling is pretty stupid. And therein lies its appeal. The audience enters into an unwritten contract with the performers: we are prepared to suspend our disbelief on the understanding that you entertain us.

I first started to write about wrestling when I launched a fanzine – this was the pre-blog era – on the subject in 1995. It coincided with the peak of what was euphemistically known as tape trading but was, in fact, little more than below-the-radar bootlegging. With the right contacts, for a few quid you could get hold of third or fourth-generation VHS copies of some of the barmiest wrestling ever conceived, from the relentless violence of cult Philadelphia outfit ECW, to masked Mexican wrestling, brutal Japanese deathmatches (fortunately a misnomer – no one ever died as a result of participating in one), to San Francisco's aptly-named Incredibly Strange Wrestling.

It was a world in which the concept of real and fake soon became an anachronism – when a man is being flung into a load of barbed wire laced with explosives, it's largely irrelevant that it's a pre-arranged stunt. This stuff was as compelling as it was weird – and, as a budding fanzine editor, I couldn't have hoped for better source material. The scribblings in my modest photocopied 'zine eventually led to a freelance writing gig with authoritative wrestling magazine *Power Slam*. But even as I began to cover the more mainstream end of the grap game, sheer oddness was never far away. The very first article I penned for the mag – a review of the WWF's annoyingly-monickered *WrestleMania X-Seven* – included an appraisal of a match during which one grappler attempted to mow down his opponent with a golf buggy.

Wrestling weirdness is not a recent phenomenon though. As you'll read, ever since the concept of pro wrestling first emerged from American carnivals in the 19th century, promoters have come up with increasingly barmy ideas in a bid to capture an audience's imagination. Matches have gone wrong (genuine injuries are far from a rarity) and grapplers have ignored the script. Occasionally, onlookers have even taken it upon themselves to get involved and transform a simulated fracas into one that's all too real: children were banned from attending cards at New York's Madison Square Garden for almost 20 years after wrestling fans at the venue rioted in the late 1950s.

But usually, professional wrestling is a performance, albeit an athletic one. (There are exceptions to this, of course – remember Big Daddy?) As such, wrestling is whatever a promoter deems it to be. Hence the tales here of the Japanese grappler who battled an alligator, Kendo Nagasaki's purported expertise at hypnosis, an exploding swimming pool, the wrestler who accidentally ended up in a real fight with Muhammad Ali, the duo who lost their tag team titles six days before they won them, a wrestling bear... and a novel use for a syringe. You'll laugh, you'll cry, you'll almost certainly wince (not least when you get to the bit about Andre the Giant shitting on his opponent). In the process, you'll uncover an alternative history of this unique form of entertainment, one that transcends boundaries of culture, age, geography, incredulity and – more often than not – taste.

I'd like to thank Paul Dyer, Phil Jones, Kieran Lefort, Grant Lowrie and Findlay Martin for their assistance during the research and writing of this book. The fact that I've finally stopped badgering people about the minutiae of bizarre wrestling matches probably comes as a relief to them all.

OVERZEALOUS FANS
3:16

CHAPTER 1:

THAT WASN'T MEANT TO HAPPEN

Las Vegas, Nevada, November 1988
South African military man thwarts double-cross – by yanking off opponent's foot

'Oh my god, I've pulled his foot off.' That was the first thing than ran through the mind of Ed Wiskoski – who portrayed the character of a violently racist South African named Colonel DeBeers – when a 1988 American Wrestling Association match against Kerry Von Erich went spectacularly awry.

At the time, the biggest secret in wrestling wasn't that the results were pre-determined. It was that Von Erich – a former NWA world champion – had lost his foot following a horrific motorcycle accident in June 1986 in Argyle, Texas, in which he crashed into the back of a police car. His right foot and ankle were crushed, and the specialists that treated him said he would never wrestle again.

But as the main draw in his father's struggling promotion, World Class Championship Wrestling, he returned to the ring months before he had fully recovered. He defeated Brian Adias in his comeback performance in February 1987 - but he was only able to make it through the match due to being given a huge shot of the local anaesthetic Novocain. During the bout he re-broke his ankle, which caused complications that led to the amputation of his foot. He eventually resumed his career with the aid of a prosthesis.

'I think for the most part, nobody knew he'd lost his foot except his family,' says Wiskoski. 'In hindsight, you can look back at the fact that he would come to the dressing room already dressed for his match and he would leave without taking a shower. It was odd but you didn't think too much about it.' Prior to his bout with Von Erich, Wiskoski was informed by Wahoo McDaniel - a fellow wrestler and also, as 'booker', the man responsible for deciding the result of the match - that it would end with the referee counting both men out of the ring. 'I could tell by talking to Von Erich that he was somewhat leery about this double count-out, not that it really made any difference,' says Wiskoski.

Once the match started, Wiskoski thought nothing further of Von Erich's misgivings. After 10 minutes of exchanges, the two combatants brawled to the ringside area, at which point they were supposed to be counted out. But, says Wiskoski, contrary to the instructions they had received from McDaniel, 'Von Erich made a mad dash to get back in the ring. I smelt a double-cross, so I just grabbed the only thing available to me, and that was his foot. And it came off in my hand.

'I was just, "Aaah!" and dropped it on the floor, wondering what had I done. Someone who was sat at ringside later said to me, "I don't know who was more shocked - Von Erich or you."' Von Erich backed out of the ring and hid his leg underneath it as he reattached his wrestling-boot-clad prosthesis. In a bid to continue the performance, Wiskoski threw a series of kicks at his prone opponent, although Von Erich did nothing to 'sell' the blows.

'He was more intent on getting that prosthesis put back on and I guess I don't blame him,' reflects Wiskoski. 'And we got counted out as per the original plan. Everybody thought it was something I had done to further my career or make him look bad, which was the farthest thing from the truth. Had I known that it was a prosthesis, I'd have either grabbed him above it or done something to get back in the ring and beat the count. But I never was told anything.'

Steve Austin vs Savio Vega

Florence, South Carolina, May 1996

SURREAL

COCK UP

Leather strap match continues in dark after storm causes power cut

A 'dark match' is wrestling industry terminology for an opening contest that isn't broadcast during an otherwise televised event. What it doesn't usually refer to is a match that literally takes place in the dark.

Even before 'Stone Cold' Steve Austin stepped in the ring to face Savio Vega at the World Wrestling Federation's curiously-titled pay-per-view *In Your House: Beware of Dog*, the two wrestlers knew they weren't in for an easy night. Their meeting would be fought under Caribbean strap match rules, in which the left wrist of each wrestler is tied to one end of a long leather strap. Audiences expect the heavy leash to be used as a weapon, and Austin and Vega both anticipated that they would end the match covered in painful welts across the upper body.

What they couldn't have known is that, two-thirds of the way through the violent confrontation, a power cut caused by a major storm would shut down the main lighting in the arena and cut the television feed to viewers at home. The result was that the entire venue was illuminated only by low-level lighting provided by an emergency generator. Even fans at ringside struggled to see what was taking place in the ring but wrestlers are taught that, whatever happens, you should respond as if you were in a real fight. So the match continued in near-darkness.

The grapplers flogged one another fiercely across the chest and back with the leather strap: even if the live audience couldn't make out what was taking place, they could at least hear the savage blows that were being delivered. After around five minutes of shadowy exchanges, Vega won the brawl, which – under strap match rules – is done by touching all four corners of the ring without losing control of the match.

By the time power was restored, there was less than half an hour of the show left, which forced the WWF – which was renamed World Wrestling Entertainment (WWE) in May 2002 – to re-run the event two days later in North Charleston. *Beware of Dog 2* consisted of the lit matches taped at the first show, along with live re-enactments of the bouts that took place in the dark (and were never broadcast). Austin and Vega repeated their sadistic performance, this time with the additional stipulation that if 'Stone Cold' lost – which, of course, he did – his manager Ted DiBiase would have to leave the WWF (he was about to sign a deal with rival group WCW). On the DVD *The Legacy of Stone Cold Steve Austin*, the goateed grappler said that he hoped the lights didn't go out for a second time 'because I don't think I have three of these things in me.'

Beware of Dog wasn't the only time a promotion ran wrestling matches in the dark. Three years earlier, gonzo Japanese outfit W*ING presented a 'lights out deathmatch' between cult hero Mitsuhiro Matsunaga and a man in a Freddy Krueger mask. The contest was illuminated only by the arena's exit lights and camera flashes and, as the two brawled through the darkened hall, it was impossible for the majority of fans to catch sight of anything – making it one of the stupidest ideas ever seen (or not seen) in a wrestling match. Krueger was declared the winner by knockout when he hung his opponent by the neck from the venue's balcony.

Rhyno vs Tajiri

Wrestling boss marches into arena and halts match following fans' chants of 'boring'

'You can't argue with Vince,' says former WWE star Terry 'Rhyno' Gerin of his onetime boss Vince McMahon. This principle was vividly demonstrated during a match he had with Yoshihiro Tajiri at an untelevised event at Uniondale's Nassau Coliseum.

Prior to the bout, the two wrestlers decided that they would improvise much of the match in the ring, as opposed to planning out the key exchanges beforehand, which is what usually happens in wrestling. But once the contest was underway, Tajiri wasn't fighting back to Gerin's satisfaction, meaning that it just looked as if he was beating him up. In order to change the pace and rile the crowd, Gerin placed his opponent in a reverse chinlock. Tajiri fought his way out twice, only for Rhyno to place him back in the hold each time. By the third chinlock, the restless audience was hating the fact that nothing was happening and responded with a rousting chant of 'boring!'

On hearing the 5,200-strong crowd vocalising their displeasure with the match, McMahon marched down to the ring, grabbed the microphone and launched into a diatribe about how dull it was. He called for the bell to be rung and demanded that the match end immediately with no conclusion (Rhyno had been scheduled to win). He then ordered both wrestlers to leave the ring so that the night's next attraction - a bikini contest - could begin.

Gerin was furious at being humiliated in front of thousands of fans and his fellow wrestlers but management simply took this as a sign that he had a bad attitude. His WWE career came to an end in April 2005 after he had a huge row with his wife at the WrestleMania 21 aftershow party and then yelled at company officials that he didn't care if he was fired. They were happy to oblige.

War Games

Winston-Salem, North Carolina, September 1998

DOOMED CONCEPT

Disastrous nine-man cage match degenerates into comedy of errors

For all the accusations that wrestling is choreographed, this chaotic match proved that, at times, it's anything but. The premise was that three teams of three wrestlers would face each other in two rings, which were surrounded by a roofed cage. The winner would receive a shot at the WCW title the following month. Throughout the contest, which headlined an event called *Fall Brawl*, the announcers emphasised that it was 'every man for himself', wholly undermining the team concept. But a breakdown in storyline logic was the least of the bout's problems.

COCK UP

INJURY

The parade of blunders began when Sting attempted to dive from one ring to the other, only to land on his head. Roddy Piper then joined proceedings and attacked his own partner, 'Diamond' Dallas Page, for reasons that were never explained, before the camera panned across to Stevie Ray, who appeared to be wedged between the two rings.

Shortly after Hulk Hogan entered the fray, copious amounts of dry ice were pumped in – indeed, there was so much of it that viewers at home could clearly hear purportedly unconscious wrestlers coughing and spluttering. As the fog cleared, face-painted wrestler Renegade materialised in the cage, pounding his chest. He had spent the entire show hidden under the ring before entering it via a trapdoor.

He promptly fell to the mat after he was thumped by Hogan, before the ring again filled with dry ice. Renegade scurried back through the trapdoor, at which point his doppelgänger The Warrior (previously the Ultimate Warrior in the WWF) pelted into the ring to attack Hogan, who fled the cage and ensured the referee locked the door behind him. The Warrior – whose sole purpose appeared to be to throw weak-looking punches at Hogan – then slid awkwardly out of the cage through a hole that he kicked in it, twisting his ankle in the process.

He was meant to chase after Hogan but, instead, was able only to hobble in comical fashion. Once he did finally catch up with the escaping 'Hulkster', Warrior tore his biceps in the ensuing brawl. Back in the ring, DDP pinned Ray to secure the title shot and end one of the most shambolic main events ever.

Buddy Wayne vs Buddy Rose

Tacoma, Washington, August 1992

Ring caves in mid-match as colossal wrestler falls to mat

The wrestlers who appeared on events promoted by the Tacoma-based Universal Independent Wrestling had one thing in common: they *hated* the ring. 'The ring was homemade,' says veteran grappler Buddy Wayne, who regularly worked for the group. 'The promoter had it made from measurements of another ring but he didn't know how it was set up underneath. There was no give to it at all: it was rock hard.' Its amateur construction also meant that it was far more fragile than most wrestling rings – as became spectacularly apparent during a 1992 bout between Wayne and the late Buddy Rose, a former WWF star who had headlined Madison Square Garden a decade earlier.

After about five minutes of action, Wayne threw Rose into the ropes to set up a dropkick. 'As soon as he hit them, you could hear the ring go,' says Wayne. 'The underneath cables popped and he stopped in his tracks. He was lucky he didn't go out backwards. You could feel that the ring was loose underneath,

Comedy

BROKEN RING

almost like a mattress. I didn't know what he wanted to do so I clotheslined him.' It was a fateful decision: Rose, who weighed around 320lbs, fell flat on to his back. As soon as he hit the mat, there was a loud crack as the boards underneath the centre of the canvas snapped.

Wayne attempted to sustain the performance by throwing a series of punches at Rose, who was, by now, prone in a deep hollow in the centre of the shattered ring. 'Buddy lay there and just laughed. He kept saying, "This is like lying in bed." I was throwing punches. I didn't know what else to do. Then Buddy goes, "Let's get out of here."' Wayne stood up unsteadily, dragged Rose off the canvas and delivered a headbutt. Rose had decided to do as much damage to the ring as possible and, again, sold the blow by falling backwards into another section of it. His landing destroyed what remained of the boards supporting the canvas, which now swung loosely in a huge crater: only the posts and the ring apron remained standing.

Wayne leapt on top of Rose and connected with more punches, as the referee frenetically called for the timekeeper to ring the bell (the match was later ruled a no contest). 'We broke every board there was,' says Wayne. 'We just had to totally improv. We were waiting for the posts to collapse on us. I had to help him get out of there because we were stuck in that thing trying to get over the edge.' After they clambered out of the collapsed structure, the two Buddys carried on brawling briefly on the floor in a bid to give the match a conclusion. Even then, their problems weren't over, thanks to the notoriously strict regulations imposed by Washington's State Athletic Commission on what it termed 'entertainment wrestling'.

'This was when the Athletic Commission was at its worst,' says Wayne. 'The commissioner watched every match from upstairs and if there was any blood or if you fought outside the ring, he'd come down and stop the match right there. So we had to be careful. I remember the commissioner saying something to Buddy about it afterwards but he just replied, "The ring broke. What do we leave the crowd with? We just walk out? We had to do something or we can kill the town." But the guy was OK with it because there was no danger to the fans.'

IMPROMPTU FINISH

Ric Flair vs Jack Veneno

Santo Domingo, Dominican Republic, January 1983

 World champion forced to improvise title change to prevent riot

In the early 1980s, the National Wrestling Alliance world heavyweight title was wrestling's premier championship. Although the belt became synonymous with the North Carolina-based Jim Crockett Promotions (the forerunner to World Championship Wrestling), it was actually the top prize for a conglomerate of promoters across America and Japan. Title changes were rare and only took place after the NWA's championship committee had voted on them. All of which made 'Nature Boy' Ric Flair's apparent title loss to Jack Veneno – a complete unknown outside his native Dominican Republic – all the more astonishing.

Flair's first NWA title reign began in September 1981 after he defeated Dusty Rhodes. His cocky bad guy routine, charismatic interviews and ability to squeeze entertaining matches out of even the most lumbering opponents made him obvious championship material. Flair first faced Jack Veneno ('Jack Venom') in the main event of a show at Santo Domingo's Palacio de los Deportes in September 1982. A stadium-full of enthusiastic fans saw Flair retain the title against the hometown hero after they fought to a time-limit draw – although the expiration of the time limit coincided with Veneno 'knocking out' Flair with a sleeper hold. The audience thought it had witnessed Veneno win the prestigious NWA strap. Fearing reprisals if the crowd discovered the truth, Flair allowed Veneno to leave the ring with the belt and give the impression that he was, indeed, the new title holder.

Buoyed by the box office receipts, Veneno – the show's promoter – hastily arranged a rematch with the 'Nature Boy'. As far as the NWA was concerned, Flair would be defending his title against Veneno for a second time. But the raucous crowd thought they were watching the hated American wrestler attempt to regain the championship. The plan was that Roddy Piper, who was Flair's second for the match, would trip Veneno, allowing Flair to pin him and walk away with the belt. But the partisan audience was so unruly that Flair sensed that a victory over Veneno would incite a riot. Flair improvised a finish and instructed Veneno to execute a piledriver (which Veneno did so clumsily that Flair had to support his own weight with a handstand) and to then pin his shoulders to the mat. This time there could be no uncertainty: Veneno had cleanly pinned the 'Nature Boy' and was, at that moment, the world's top pro wrestler.

As the referee raised the local hero's arm and Flair raced back to the dressing room, fans piled into the ring in celebration and lifted Veneno on to their shoulders – oblivious to the fact that the contest would never be acknowledged outside the country. Veneno returned the championship to Flair backstage and subsequently appeared on the Saturday afternoon wrestling programme *Lucha Libre Internacional* (the Dominican Republic's highest-rated TV show at the time) to say that he had forfeited the title as defending it would mean he would have to leave the country. The apparent title switch was never acknowledged in the US and, to this day, the NWA does not recognise Veneno as a former champion.

Whoooooo!

Royal Rumble

Fresno, California, January 2005

Bungled ending of main event leaves WWE boss unable to stand

It's difficult to conceive how the finishing sequence of the 2005 *Royal Rumble* could have been any more botched. The highlight of WWE's annual spandex-packed spectacle was a 30-man bout in which grapplers were eliminated only after they had been flung over the top rope to the floor. After 50 minutes of sweaty action, just two men remained: John Cena and Batista. The plan was that Batista would attempt to execute his trademark sit-down powerbomb finisher, from which Cena would escape - only to subsequently capitulate to the move when Batista attempted it for a second time. Batista would then dump Cena out of the ring to win the match.

But as Cena attempted to wriggle out of the first powerbomb attempt, Batista lost his balance, causing both pseudo-combatants to tumble to the ringside area simultaneously. Unsure of how to proceed, the multiple referees involved in the bout argued over who had won in order to stall for time as they awaited further instructions.

In a bid to resolve the controversy, a furious-looking Vince McMahon - WWE chairman and himself an occasional wrestler - stomped out from the backstage area, where he had been overseeing the live pay-per-view event. As he slid into the squared circle, he caught his knee on the edge of the ring and tore two tendons in his right quadriceps muscle. With the injury leaving him unable to stand, McMahon was forced to sit on the mat as he passed on directions for a new, impromptu ending to the show. The match was then restarted and - as per the original plan - Batista chucked his nemesis to the floor in order to claim victory.

Vince McMahon additionally tore his *left* quadriceps muscle later that night when he endeavoured to walk unaided. He underwent surgery the following day, after which he had to use a wheelchair for two months.

Wladek Kowalski vs Yukon Eric

Montreal, Canada, October 1952

Wrestler loses ear after top-rope kneedrop goes horrifically awry

Yukon Eric against Wladek Kowalski was the archetypal confrontation between good and evil. Eric Holmback played the role of a hard-working lumberjack, who happened to be the strongest man in the world. Kowalski, meanwhile, portrayed a vicious maniac.

One of his signature moves was a kneedrop off the top rope, all the more impressive given his 6ft 6in height. During their match, Kowalski trapped Eric's leg in the ropes and then launched himself on to his prone opponent. Having performed the move numerous times before, he knew that the safest way to perform it was to aim for Eric's chest. But just as he was about to land, the counterfeit lumberjack attempted to roll out of the way, which resulted in Kowalski's shinbone hitting Yukon's heavily-cauliflowered left ear and slicing it off.

Referee Sammy Mack inadvertently trod on the severed appendage before picking it up and placing it in his pocket. It was, he said, still quivering. Yukon Eric was clearly unable to continue and Kowalski was declared the winner. An incredible amount of blood spurted from Eric's head - some reports state that it was hitting fans at ringside - and a towel used to stem the flow was quickly soaked bright red.

Kowalski was good friends with Eric away from the squared circle and visited him in hospital the next day. The sight of his bandaged head reminded Kowalski of Humpty Dumpty and he started chortling. A reporter from the local paper was there at the same time and ran a story about how the heinous grappler had gone to the hospital to laugh at what he'd done. The injury was a complete accident but Kowalski asserted that it had been intentional: the press dubbed him Killer Kowalski and his career was made.

Nightstalker vs Sid Vicious

Jacksonville, Florida, November 1990

Clueless rookie has one of worst matches ever on live TV special

For years after his 1986 debut, Sid Vicious (real name Sid Eudy and nothing to do with the Sex Pistols bassist) was heralded as 'the next Hulk Hogan'. Thanks to his sheer size (he was 6ft 7in tall) and impressive physique, he certainly had the look of the archetypal American pro wrestler. But he was never able to capture fans' imaginations in the way that the phenomenally successful 'Hulkster' was able to during his 1980s peak.

This was partly due to his inability to trash-talk in a convincing fashion, and partly due to his unmitigated lack of in-ring prowess – as demonstrated by the abomination of a match he had with Bryan 'Nightstalker' Clark at WCW's *Clash of the Champions XIII*.

Clark – who subsequently went on to perform for the WWF as Adam Bomb – had only wrestled a handful of matches at the time. 'I sort of got in it without any training,' he says, 'not even the basics. [Former wrestler] Ox Baker just taught me a couple of things in his living room. I didn't know how to do anything, really, other than to pound a guy.'

As the more experienced worker of the two, it was Eudy's role to help guide the rookie grappler through the match, something at which he failed spectacularly. Every element of the contest looked comically hokey. Early in the mercifully brief encounter, Clark executed a bear hug on Vicious, who made no effort to sell the pain that was supposedly being inflicted on him. Nightstalker froze, before he very clearly discussed with Eudy what they were going to do next.

Vicious clonked his opponent around the head to escape the hold, only for 'Stalker to place him back into it (although Eudy did at least make out that the embrace was causing him some discomfort second time around). Clark tentatively followed up with a series of phoney-looking knees and elbows: it quickly became apparent that this was the full extent of his arsenal. Panicking, he then pressed his palms into Sid's upper back. One can only assume that this was supposed to represent some form of dangerous nerve hold. In fact, it gave the appearance that he was providing Sid with nothing so deadly as a deep muscle massage.

As Eudy retaliated with a back suplex – at last, a proper wrestling manoeuvre – another wrestler named 'Big Cat' Curtis Hughes walked down to the ring for no apparent reason. In the confusion, Vicious struck Clark with a plastic executioner's axe and pinned him. In contradiction of wrestling lore, Clark completely forgot to give the impression that he had been damaged by the blow and stood straight back up. He briefly joined Hughes in pretending to hammer Vicious, who finally rolled out of the ring to end the fiasco.

'The little thing with me and Sid?' remembers Clark. 'I was stepping in way over my head but I wanted to get in the business. It was a terrible match but, like I said, I hadn't been trained. I didn't know what I was doing.'

Tornado elimination match

Tijuana, Mexico, October 1997

Mexican wrestlers flee to dressing room after being attacked by fans

The good guy/bad guy divide is taken very seriously by fans in Mexico, which is one of the reasons why the country is regarded as one of the more dangerous locations for a pro wrestler to earn a living. Push the ringside faithful too far and their reactions are likely to be more than just vocal. Hence the aftermath of a 16-man tornado elimination bout that took place in Tijuana's Promo Azteca in October 1997.

After Lizmark Jr pinned Psicosis to end the high-flying, 45-minute scrap, the ring was overrun by members of the heel team, who committed the ultimate lucha libre (Mexican wrestling) sin of unmasking national hero El Hijo del Santo. One ringsider vaulted the barrier in a bid to attack the heinous 'rudos' but, wisely, quickly retreated back to the stands when a wrestler named Damien charged after him.

As then-hated villain Rey Misterio Jr (later Rey Mysterio in WWE) paraded around the ring on the shoulders of uncle Rey Misterio Sr and Konnan, while holding Santo's mask aloft, the fans were unable to contain their anger at such insulting behaviour. The barrage of rubbish that was already being thrown turned into dozens of flying chairs and, when one landed on Rey Sr, he hit back at the fan responsible before legging it to the dressing room under a hail of furniture. He was closely followed by Konnan and Rey Jr, who had to fight their way through the irate audience.

Michael Myers & Leatherface vs Freddy Krueger & Crypt Keeper

Kawasaki, Japan, November 1993

Tempestuous siblings throw out script and publicly quit promotion in ring

Once the grappletainment of choice for die-hard Japanese wrestling fans, by late 1993 W*ING (Wrestling's International New Generation) had degenerated into a hammy and increasingly desperate-looking organisation. Sure, the outfit's match quality had always sucked but, where once there was blood, balcony dives and barbed wire, there was now a low-budget roster made up of third-rate performers clad in cheap horror masks.

Thus Tennessee-born brothers Doug and Eddie Gilbert found themselves on a two-week tour with the lowbrow group as masked characters Freddy Krueger and Michael Myers. It wasn't destined to be a crowning moment on their CVs as the siblings decided, a week in, to publicly quit - in the middle of a tag match.

While Doug (as Freddy Krueger) was booked to win following a wild brawl, as part of the build-up to a spike nail deathmatch between Krueger and Leatherface that was due to take place two months later, he instead allowed Eddie (as Michael Myers) to pin him after only 13 seconds. The match would have been even quicker but Eddie's first attempt at pinning Doug came to naught, as the referee refused to count the fall due to the fact that the opening bell hadn't rung.

The duo then removed their masks and, over the PA, castigated the promotion as being a 'piece of shit' and pledged their allegiance to rival troupe All Japan Pro Wrestling, before Eddie yelled at confused ringside fans to leave the building. The brothers flew home the next morning and, unsurprisingly, never worked for W*ING again.

Shane Douglas vs Too Cold Scorpio

DOUBLE CROSS

Philadelphia, Pennsylvania, August 1994

Tournament victor goes heroically off-message and rubbishes the very title he's just won

By 1994, the National Wrestling Alliance – once the most powerful wrestling organisation in North America – consisted of just six members representing small-time promotions. And thanks to WCW's withdrawal from the conglomerate, it also had no champion. After almost a year of being little more than a paper organisation, the group decided to crown a new title holder with an eight-man, one-night tournament that would be hosted by Philadelphia's Eastern Championship Wrestling.

The NWA board (which consisted of just three people) was keen to award the gold to Chris Benoit but ECW owner Tod Gordon petitioned for ECW's then-champion 'The Franchise' Shane Douglas to win the tournament. The NWA acquiesced on the understanding that Douglas would lose the belt to Benoit shortly after the tournament took place. Gordon agreed to the terms with the NWA's Dennis Coraluzzo – knowing full well that a Douglas/Benoit NWA title match would never happen.

Douglas met Too Cold Scorpio in the tourney final, which went ahead as designed: after 12 minutes of exchanges, Scorpio missed a splash off the top rope, Douglas executed a belly-to-belly suplex and secured the three-count. He had done nothing to betray what would happen next.

He was handed the title by Coraluzzo and, with the belt slung over his shoulder, stood in the centre of the ring and began to speak into the microphone.

As the crowd applauded respectfully, 'The Franchise' listed a number of renowned former NWA champions, including Lou Thesz, Jack Brisco, Harley Race and Ric Flair. But rather than praise the retro grapplers, he instead proclaimed that they could all 'kiss my ass' and flung the NWA gold to the mat. He then grabbed his ECW belt – which was, until this point, considered as nothing more than a regional championship – and declared himself the ECW heavyweight champion of the world as a dumbfounded Coraluzzo looked on.

Gordon and ECW booker Paul Heyman had planned the deception for several weeks in a bid to garner notoriety for the upstart promotion and distance itself from the old-school NWA, which Heyman considered to be a 'bunch of nobodies'. The fact that it also gave Gordon the opportunity to ridicule Coraluzzo, with whom he had been in a bitter promotional battle, only served to make the scheme even more appealing. Coraluzzo had actually been tipped off that a double-cross was in the works and had considered scrapping the tournament but, ultimately, paid no heed to the warning.

Backstage, Heyman told Coraluzzo that what he had just witnessed was simply a storyline to generate interest in Douglas as champion and that a stage-managed NWA/ECW feud would benefit both organisations. Heyman even convinced Coraluzzo to record an interview for ECW's TV show, in which he branded Douglas a 'disgrace' but stated that he was still the NWA champion 'whether he likes it or not'. But in the same episode, which was broadcast three days after the tournament, Gordon announced that ECW was quitting the NWA, would be renamed Extreme Championship Wrestling and recognised Douglas as the ECW world champion.

Coraluzzo realised that he had been played for a second time and released a statement declaring the title tournament null and void, although it seemed a bit late for that really. The NWA held a second title tournament in November, which was won by Chris Candido. But the once-prestigious championship was, by now, little more than a glorified indie belt, as demonstrated by the fact that it was later held by such no-names as Mike Rapada and Brit wrestler Gary Steele. ECW, the self-styled outlaw promotion, secured a sizeable cult following, if not the cash flow to match it, and went bust in January 2001 with debts of almost $7.5 million (Shane Douglas alone was owed $48,000). Its assets were later purchased by WWE, which revived the brand in 2005.

Eric Young vs Johnny Devine Orlando, Florida, August 2006

Wrestling venue evacuated when it catches fire during live television broadcast

It was a spectacular start to a wrestling show - albeit for the wrong reasons. To herald the beginning of the live television broadcast of TNA's *Hard Justice* event, a dazzling fireworks display was triggered, a common motif of American pay-per-views. The fireworks reached the top of the building, a soundstage at Universal Studios in Orlando, and set fire to a hessian sack that was wrapped around a pipe just below the ceiling.

Wrestlers Eric Young and Johnny Devine entered the ring, oblivious to the small fire that was burning above their heads. After only a few minutes of action, the crowd spotted plumes of smoke pouring from the ceiling and chanted, 'The roof, the roof, the roof is on fire!' The referee looked up pensively as the two grapplers continued with the contest.

In a bid to contain the blaze, staff raced up to the rafters and blasted the flames with fire extinguishers. This succeeded in snuffing out the fire but also produced a huge cloud of dry powder that descended into the ring. The wrestlers were barely able to see each other through the fog and, worse, were having difficulty breathing (Young later said that the discharge tasted of salt and vinegar crisps). Ringside fans, in between choking, began a chant of, 'You can't see us!' Despite the entertainment venue now bearing more resemblance to the set of a disaster movie, Young and Devine were given no instructions to end the match and continued with it as best they could - even though the drama of the building being on fire was far more gripping than what was taking place in the ring.

In the midst of the dense fog, viewers were just able to make out Devine choking Young against the bottom rope, before the wrestlers staggered around the ring. Devine then threw some punches and, while waiting for the mist to disperse, stalled by talking trash at Young. The ring finally began to clear and the match concluded as intended when Young pinned Devine following a modified neckbreaker.

But TNA's problems weren't over, as the fire department ordered the premises to be evacuated so it could inspect the damage. As fans filed outside, announcers Mike Tenay and Don West stalled for time by previewing the rest of the night's matches. When they too were ordered from the building, a video package hyping the main event of Sting against Jeff Jarrett was played on a loop for over 10 minutes. Cameras eventually cut to Tenay and ring announcer Jeremy Borash, who continued the broadcast from outside the venue. As firefighters scurried about in the background, they interviewed a succession of grapplers, including Eric Young, who protested that he didn't start the fire. After 20 minutes, everyone was allowed back into the building and the show resumed as if nothing had happened.

Wrestling venue catches fire on live TV

Hart Foundation vs The Rockers

BROKEN RING

Fort Wayne, Indiana, October 1990

TV executives compel WWF tag title change to be excised from history

When is a title change not a title change? When the top rope breaks – according to the WWF, at least. In the autumn of 1990, WWF honcho Vince McMahon decided that the team of Bret 'Hitman' Hart and Jim 'The Anvil' Neidhart, collectively the Hart Foundation, had run its course. The duo, he decreed, would lose the WWF tag titles to The Rockers (Marty Jannetty and Shawn Michaels). This would precede Hart receiving a major promotional push as a singles wrestler, while Neidhart would be phased out of the ring and employed instead as a commentator – a role, incidentally, for which he was spectacularly ill-suited.

The title change would take place at a taping for an NBC TV special and, to add to the occasion, would be fought under best-of-three-falls rules. During the bout's second session, Neidhart accidentally detached the top rope from the turnbuckle, which was reaffixed by the ring crew prior to the start of the third fall. Jannetty went on to pin Neidhart, as planned, to win the final fall and secure the WWF tag belts, in a total time of 25 minutes.

Prior to the broadcast of the show three weeks later, NBC informed the WWF that it only required a 60-minute programme, in contrast to the show's usual 90-minute slot. The lengthy tag match wouldn't fit on the broadcast without being heavily edited and so was removed completely. McMahon then second-guessed his decision to promote The Rockers to tag champs and break up the Hart Foundation, and the belts were returned to Hart and Neidhart a few days later. The Rockers' title victory never aired and the WWF retrospectively claimed the match was negated due to the broken ring.

Christian vs William Regal

Montreal, Canada, September 2009

Announcer confuses grappler with guitarist from 1980s indie band The Smiths

Wrestling commentators have a peculiarly narrow field of reference that generally extends no further than other American sports (in a misguided attempt to legitimise the grap game) and comedy shows from the 1970s (which is when many of them appeared to have last taken an active interest in popular culture).

WWE announcer Matt Striker decided to take a more esoteric approach during his voice-over for the confrontation between ECW champion Christian and William Regal at an event dubbed *Breaking Point* – by crowbarring in as many references to sardonic Manchester singer Morrissey and his former band The Smiths as possible.

To begin with, the citations were imperceptibly subtle, such as when he referred to Regal as 'maladjusted' (the title of a 1997 Morrissey album that peaked at number 61 in the US charts). But as Striker's confidence increased, so did the surreal nature of his banter. When Regal kneed his foe in the face, Striker commented, 'Ask the question, "How soon is now?"' (the title of a 1985 single by The Smiths). This was rapidly followed by the observation that, 'Everyday is like Sunday [an allusion to Morrissey's second solo single] for the number one contender William Regal.'

At least when the challenger thumped Christian with his left hand, Striker's remark of 'southpaw grammar [a 1995 Morrissey album] from William Regal' was based on some sort of logic. Something that can't be said of his follow-up: 'Johnny Marr [The Smiths' guitarist] just looking to rearrange the facial features of the ECW champion.' Shortly before he won the match, the defending champion clocked Regal in the face with an elbow, at which point Striker name-checked Morrissey's 2004 comeback album and exclaimed, 'You are the quarry!'

Andre the Giant, El Canek & Dos Caras vs Bad News Allen, Bam Bam Bigelow & Kokina Maximus

Mexico City, Mexico, December 1992

Inebriated giant loses control of bowels in middle of match

Andre the Giant's drinking career was as illustrious as his wrestling one. A story on the 6ft 10in-tall grappler in the December 1981 issue of *Sports Illustrated* listed a typical daily consumption of a case of beer, two bottles of wine, up to eight shots of brandy, around six Bloody Marys and the occasional glass of Pernod. The notorious booze-hound is also reported to have downed 14 bottles of wine prior to his *WrestleMania III* main event with Hulk Hogan. So central was drinking to

Andre's existence that nothing could force him to abstain: not even a serious stomach upset.

Andre was in Mexico in December 1992 for a one-off match for the Universal Wrestling Association. He had been tormented all day by terrible stomach cramps and diarrhoea but insisted that he would still be able to participate in his scheduled six-man tag match. On top of the stomach complaint, he continued to indulge in his usual extended drinking session. It didn't help matters.

Midway through the bout, he faced off against Bad News Allen (better known as Bad News Brown during his 1988-1990 WWF tenure). Andre was dictating what would happen in the ring, known in the trade as 'calling the spots'. As he threw Bad News into the corner, he muttered to him, 'Big ass, boss.' (Andre called everyone 'boss'.) This verbal shorthand told Allen to remain slumped in the corner as Andre was about to hit him with one of his trademark moves, in which he would turn his back to his opponent, grab hold of the ropes and - there's no delicate way to put this - thrust his enormous arse into his adversary, supposedly crushing him in the corner.

The combination of the collision and the copious volume of booze he had taken on board meant that, as soon as Andre hit Bad News, he lost any control he once had over his bowels. Liquid faeces dribbled out of his wrestling singlet and all over Allen's chest. Bad News fell out of the ring and, resisting the urge to throw up, pelted back to the dressing room. His tag team partners continued the contest without him, once they'd finished laughing at his predicament. As Bad News passed fans on his way backstage, they shouted, 'Wow, what is that smell?' having presumably never been confronted by a wrestler covered in diarrhoea before.

Bad News jumped straight into the showers, while still wearing his wrestling trunks and boots, in a bid to clean himself up. But despite having been shat upon by a giant, he remained remarkably sanguine about the incident. 'I felt sorry for the guy,' he later said. 'He was just sick, that's all.' The match proved to be one of Andre's last prior to his death at the age of 46 on 27 January 1993 from congestive heart failure, which was caused by his untreated acromegaly, the glandular disease that resulted in his enormous size.

GENUINE
POW
FIGHT
WRESTLI
COCK
BLOOD
DOUBLE
CROSS
DOOMED
CONCEPT
WATER
SURREAL
EPIC

CHAPTER 2:

THE PIONEERS

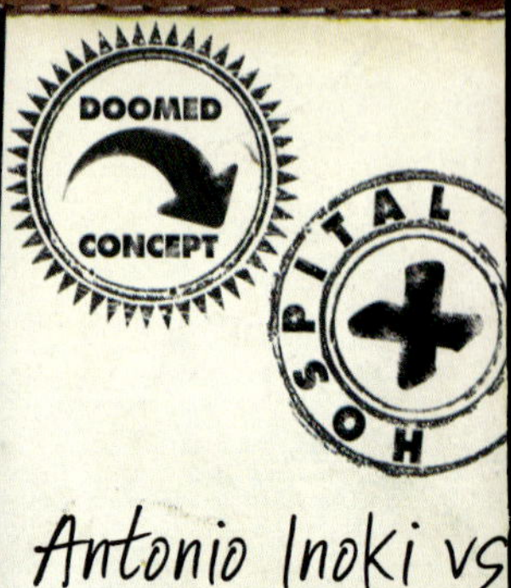

Antonio Inoki vs Muhammad Ali

Tokyo, Japan, June 1976

Japanese wrestler survives fight with greatest boxer ever by refusing to get up off mat

Antonio Inoki's collision with Muhammad Ali is the most famous match in Japanese pro wrestling history – and probably the worst. Inoki was the founder and top star of New Japan Pro Wrestling, one of the country's two dominant wrestling promotions during the 1970s-1990s. At the time, wrestlers were considered to be among the toughest sportsmen in Japan. Inoki played on this by matching himself against fighters from other disciplines, a concept that pre-dated the rise of mixed martial arts organisations such as UFC by almost two decades.

In the first of these matches, which took place in February 1976, Inoki defeated Willem Ruska – who won a judo gold medal at the 1972 Olympics – in a 20-minute fight. Despite Ruska's legitimate credentials, the result was pre-determined, which was also the plan for Inoki's next mixed contest, in which he would face three-time heavyweight boxing champion Muhammad Ali. The Japanese wrestler would bolster his celebrity status with a victory over the most famous sportsman ever in a match at Tokyo's Budokan Hall on 25 June

1976. In return, Ali would receive a pay-off of $6 million, which was larger than any purse he had received at that point for a boxing match. At least, that was the plan when he signed for the fight in March 1976.

Promoter Bob Arum said that the original script called for Ali to pummel Inoki for six or seven rounds, by which point blood would be streaming down the Japanese wrestler's face. Ali would then plead with the referee to stop the fight, only for his opponent to attack him from behind and pin him.

Ali arrived in Tokyo on 16 June. A lunch party at which both athletes were present served as the first media event. The boxer unleashed one of his trademark verbal tirades: 'You'll make $4 million because you're meeting the world's most famous man and the world's prettiest athlete!' Inoki responded, 'We would be delighted to take you on as our publicity man when the fight is over,' before he handed Ali a gift-wrapped crutch.

But just two days before the fight was due to take place, 'The Greatest' decided that he didn't want to deceive the public by losing a fixed match and refused to attend any of the rehearsals. The only way to appease Ali's conscience was to make the bout a genuine wrestler vs boxer battle – albeit one with rules that hugely favoured 'The Louisville Lip' after he had watched one of Inoki's sparring sessions and realised that he would be defenceless against many of the wrestler's manoeuvres.

Inoki was subsequently banned from using tackle-style takedowns, kicks above the waist, punches, suplexes and submission holds. If he did manage to take Ali down to the mat, he would have 20 seconds in which to score a pinfall before both fighters would be stood up again by the referee. If Ali could grab the ropes, it would also result in a stand-up. As a consequence of such prohibitive rules, Inoki spent most of the 15-round encounter on his back, kicking at Ali's legs. This was actually a shrewd tactic given the regulations imposed on him. Ali didn't throw his first punch until the seventh round and he threw a total of only six punches, of which two landed, during the entire 45-minute time-limit draw. It was one of the most tedious encounters ever.

As dull as the match was for the audience, Ali's legs nonetheless took a legitimate pounding and he was later hospitalised for weeks with two blood clots and muscle damage. Ali later received just $2.1 million of his agreed fee, largely due to the lower than expected revenue that was generated by the closed-circuit broadcast of the fight in the US. The match was derided as a farce but, in Japan at least, is now viewed as a precursor to modern mixed martial arts and helped to cement Inoki's status as a cultural icon.

Argentina Rocca & Edouard Carpentier vs Dick the Bruiser & Dr Jerry Graham

New York, November 1957

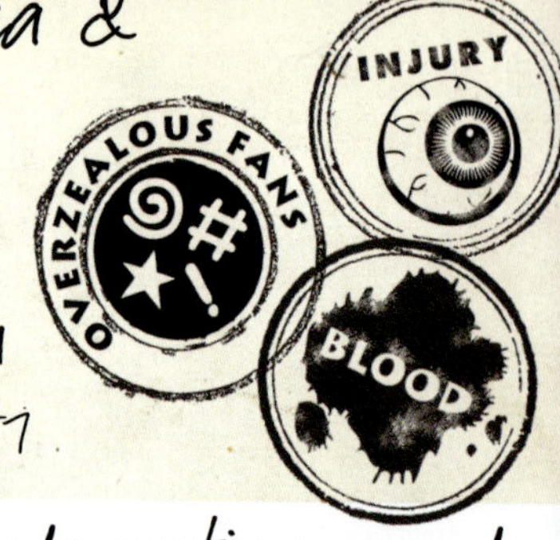

Bad-guy tag team goads partisan crowd, which responds with full-scale riot

Part of the role for any self-respecting villain (or 'heel' in wrestling parlance) is to antagonise and rile the audience. One indication that you may have taken this too far is when you manage to provoke the crowd into unrestrained rioting, which is what happened after the culmination of a tag team main event at New York's Madison Square Garden in November 1957.

Antonino 'Argentina' Rocca was a hugely popular local favourite whose matches sold out the famed arena over 20 times – so the audience was delighted when he won the first fall for his team by defeating Dick 'The Bruiser' Afflis with his trademark backbreaker. When the heels recovered during the second fall and dominated Rocca by using illegal double-team tactics, the 13,000-strong audience's euphoria turned to agitation. The assault on Rocca continued until he began to bleed from the head which, in accordance with the narrative that had been planned for the encounter, caused him to become so enraged that he ferociously pummelled Graham's cranium against the ring post.

By this point, the referee had disqualified the nefarious duo of Graham and 'The Bruiser', ostensibly bringing an end to proceedings. But spectators were so roused by Rocca's apparently spontaneous example of violence that two members of the audience – one of whom brandished an umbrella – rushed the ring, presumably in an ill-conceived bid to aid Rocca and Carpentier in battering their rivals. Afflis fended off the charging spectators, while an undeterred Rocca continued with the performance and carried on pounding Graham.

The chaos quickly escalated: hundreds of fans surged towards the ring, while others ran for the exits as bottles and beer cans hailed down from the balcony. In the commotion, fights broke out in the aisles. Graham and Bruiser fled to the dressing room; somewhat belatedly, Rocca attempted to calm his fans, who instead paraded him around the ringside area on their shoulders. The riot – during which 300 chairs were damaged – was only quelled after a 30-man police detail dashed to the arena. Two cops were injured – one after he was hit in the head with a bottle, the other after he fell off a ramp – while two men were charged with disorderly conduct for fighting and throwing chairs. An inexplicably tolerant police captain later pointed out that 'these people are just naturally emotional'.

All four wrestlers were hauled in front of the State Athletic Commission three days later, where they were fined a total of $2,600. The commission's chairman, Julius Helfand, cancelled the next wrestling event at the Garden and also decreed that future cards would be allowed only one tag team contest each due to the fact that, as one newspaper report put it at the time, 'More than one such exhibition a night excited the fans too much.' He also banned children under 14 from attending wrestling shows at the venue – a ruling that wasn't overturned until almost 20 years later.

El Santo vs Enrique Llanes

Defeated grappler avoids stipulated head shaving after fans trap him in dressing room

In Mexican wrestling or lucha libre (literally, 'free fighting'), the ultimate feud-ender is a match in which each luchadore stakes either his mask or hair. It's a stipulation that is always honoured, to the extent that the Mexican boxing and wrestling commission will fine wrestlers who continue to wear their masks in the ring after losing such a match.

Enrique Llanes, one of 14 children, grew up idolising wrestling champion Tarzán López. He became a locksmith but never lost his love of the mat game and once had a chance meeting with López on his way back from work. Somewhat implausibly, López - the country's top grappling star at the time - agreed to train Llanes in exchange for Llanes teaching him how to be a locksmith (López opened a successful chain of key-cutting shops after he retired from lucha libre).

Llanes began his career in June 1942 as a preliminary wrestler who appeared every Sunday at Arena Mexico - the country's premier wrestling venue - in either the first or second match on the card. To begin with, he always lost but gradually became a cult favourite, which led to him being moved further up the billing and into feuds with headline acts such as Sugi Sito, Gori Guerrero (Llanes' brother-in-law) and El Santo, at the time a hated villain.

The feud between Llanes and Santo culminated in a mask vs hair contest. As per the script, Llanes lost the confrontation after an epic struggle. The audience was so moved by his performance that they 'forgave' him for the loss and didn't want to see him lose his hair. A group of zealous ringsiders charged into the ring and carried Llanes aloft to the backstage area to prevent the barber from delivering the promised mop chop.

Mexico City, Mexico, July 1949

Promoter Francisco Flores ordered the defeated grappler to return to the ring and have his head shaved. But the crowd was having none of it and physically blocked the aisle so that Llanes was unable to leave the dressing room area. When he arrived home later that night, his elderly mother started to cry as she thought that he had unmasked El Santo. When he told her what had happened, she forced him to cut his hair off immediately in order to honour the stipulation. Fans remembered Llanes' outstanding performance in the match and he remained a top star in Mexico for the next decade.

As for El Santo (real name Rodolfo Guzmán Huerta), he went on to become Mexico's most popular wrestler ever and one of the country's biggest film stars, playing the lead in over 50 campy movies as the silver mask-clad hero. An estimated crowd of 10,000 filled the streets of Mexico City in a bid to glimpse his coffin on its way to his funeral in February 1984. He never lost his mask in the ring and was clad in it when he was buried.

Joe Stecher vs Ed Lewis

Omaha, Nebraska, July 1916

Fearsome submission expert bores fans with dreary five-hour stalemate

This match between intense rivals Joe Stecher and Ed 'Strangler' Lewis must have been as painful for the live audience to watch as it was for the wrestlers to perform. While WWE occasionally promotes 60-minute 'iron man' matches, such contests don't come close to rivalling the duration of this epic – and intensely dull – early 20th-century battle.

At the time, professional wrestling was still in the formative stages of development and was less than a generation removed from its sideshow roots, where trained fighters would take on members of the audience in legitimate scraps. Wrestlers and promoters alike were deeply paranoid that, if the paying public discovered that the mat game no longer equated to authentic competition, business would tank overnight. As such, they were prepared to – quite literally – go to incredible lengths to protect the industry.

One of the ways in which this was done was by presenting inordinately long main events, as audiences equated protracted stalemates with genuine contests. Such promotional tactics were pushed to the outer limits of credulity in this 1916 bout, which began at 1.30pm: after five hours of exchanges, during which Lewis spent much of the time stalling, the match was declared a draw. Lewis's manager Billy Sandow subsequently claimed that, while Stecher was hospitalised after the match, Lewis 'had a light supper and danced until 4.30 the next morning.'

The 'Strangler' went on to beat Stecher in December 1920 to win his first undisputed world title. The submission specialist later decried the development of faster-paced matches based around more exciting (albeit less realistic) manoeuvres as 'terrible slambang wrestling'.

BLOOD

Rikidozan, Toyonobori & Great Togo vs Freddie Blassie, Lou Thesz & Mike Sharpe

Kobe, Japan, April 1962

Scornful bad guy's sadistic assault causes TV viewers to suffer fatal heart attacks

Freddie Blassie was never what you would call a mat technician. Where other grapplers of his era would employ headlocks and side suplexes, Blassie preferred the more straightforward approach of punching, biting and choking. During his first Japanese tour in April 1962, he quickly ascended to the position of the most hated wrestler in the country. His cause was helped significantly by the fact that he had seven teeth capped, which he would then hone into sharp points with a nail file during television interviews.

So notorious was Blassie for using his sharpened gnashers to wound adversaries that he was nicknamed 'The Vampire' – a monicker he lived up to during a six-man tag bout that took place at the Ohji Gym in Kobe, Japan's fifth-largest city. During the match, which was broadcast live on national television station NTV, close-up shots were shown of Blassie – with a maniacal glint in his eye – biting into the Great Togo's head and of the subsequent profuse blood loss. The images were so shocking that six elderly men who were watching the match on TV suffered fatal heart attacks.

Blassie, the consummate heel, would later inflate the figure exponentially and boasted that he had caused 92 Japanese viewers to die during his career. 'My ambition was to kill 100 and I failed,' he said. As a result of the match, Blassie became a huge celebrity in Japan and, even though it was the country's most-watched programme at the time, wrestling was almost banned from television.

Kendo Nagasaki & Blondie Barrett vs Steve Regal & Robbie Brookside

Bedworth, UK, August 1988

Masked villain overcomes two-against-one handicap by hypnotising opponent

To modern eyes, British wrestling of the late 1980s is a peculiar concept, consisting as it did of normal-looking blokes (Giant Haystacks notwithstanding) in swimming trunks, exchanging overhand wristlocks in provincial town halls. But this best-of-three-falls tag team match – which was taped in August 1988 but not broadcast on ITV until October – was odder still than most UK main events.

The star of the match was Kendo Nagasaki, the enigmatic, samurai-inspired mat man clad in a distinctly homemade-looking mask adorned with horizontal white stripes. Nagasaki and regular tag partner Blondie Barrett – whose imaginative name was based on the fact of his blond hair – dominated the slender Brookside in the first session, during which it became apparent that Nagasaki's repertoire was largely limited to jabbing his fingers in his opponent's throat. 'Nagasaki a master of that move,' noted commentator Kent Walton, dryly.

After Nagasaki pinned Brookside to take the first fall, Brookside equalised when he knocked Blondie down to the mat for a count of 10 with a dropkick off the top. Barrett not only lost the fall, the referee decreed that he was not allowed to take any further part in the match. The purpose of this seemingly arbitrary ruling soon became apparent. Contrary to the prevailing wrestling plot device in which the fan favourite heroically battles the odds, the final stanza saw the iniquitous Nagasaki at a two-on-one disadvantage. Many viewers may have assumed that even Kendo couldn't overcome such hostile statistics. But that would be to overlook his mysterious mind control abilities. Steve Regal (later William Regal in the WWF/WWE) and Brookside double-teamed their opponent, before Brookside hit him with a top-rope dropkick – the same move that had already beaten Blondie. Crucially, Nagasaki wasn't knocked out by the impact but it did give Brookside the opportunity to peel off the apparently helpless Nagasaki's mask to reveal a chubby-faced man with a prominent nose and a black horse's tail of hair growing out of the back of his otherwise bald head.

'And there he is, Nagasaki as we haven't seen him before,' said Walton, conveniently forgetting that Kendo performed a much-vaunted ceremonial unmasking during a televised event 11 years earlier. Brookside had done nothing but fall for Kendo's ruse though: Nagasaki grabbed his young opponent by the shoulders, stared intently into his eyes and waved his hands around in a manner that vaguely approximated the movements of a stage hypnotist. Brookside – who was now looking straight ahead gormlessly – had to simulate being under Nagasaki's hypnotic spell, in front of a baying crowd in a civic hall just north of Coventry. It's a testament to his dedication to the mat game that he didn't burst out laughing.

Nagasaki grabbed his mask off Brookside and placed it back over his head, before he yelled indecipherably and pointed at the corner in which Regal was standing. Brookside ambled towards his partner, punched him in the stomach, dragged him into the ring by his hair and then, for good measure, clouted him around the head. Nagasaki concluded the assault on Regal with a rolling fireman's carry slam, after which the referee counted the future WWF star down for 10, handing the once-again-masked man the victory. Kendo then sauntered over to Brookside and flapped his hands in front of his face, whereupon Brookside snapped out of the trance – something he signified by shaking his head and rubbing his eyes in a comically overstated fashion.

Brookside finally regained enough composure to seize the microphone, into which he blurted, 'Hey, referee, that man's just done something to me.' But despite his allegation of foul play, the ruling stood. Two months after the match was broadcast, ITV cancelled British wrestling.

Mr Wrestling vs Arnold Spurling

Columbus, Georgia, 1967

Masked suplex specialist loses finger in fight with audience member

MISSING BODY PART

OVERZEALOUS FANS

Ridiculous as it now sounds, the embryonic version of pro wrestling in the second half of the 19th century consisted of trained grapplers taking on members of the audience - lured by the promise of a cash prize if they won - in legitimate scraps at travelling carnivals. Promoters would make their money from the bets placed on the local heroes: with their arsenals of excruciating armlocks and efficient chokes, the sideshow wrestlers rarely lost.

By the early 1900s, there was more money to be made from selling tickets for the spectacle of worked bouts, and the challenge matches of pro wrestling's formative years became little more than a historical curio. The gimmick was occasionally revived though, most notably by Mr Wrestling when he debuted in the Georgia territory in 1967 and offered $1,000 to any fan who could last 10 minutes with him. Under the white mask was former amateur wrestling champion Tim Woods, who was confident that his legitimate grappling credentials would enable him to fend off the chancers who stepped in the ring with him.

But when he faced Arnold Spurling - a local hard man who was determined to expose wrestling as fake - the brawl went horribly wrong. Spurling suckerpunched Woods, ripped his mask off and threw it into the crowd. Woods hid his face in his hands until the mask was returned to him by the referee. With his disguise back in place, he took Spurling down to the canvas, where he was able to use his wrestling skills to subdue his excitable adversary. Spurling retaliated by biting one of the masked man's fingers off at the first joint and spitting the digit on to the mat. An understandably miffed Woods pummelled Spurling with kicks to the face, before he was whisked off to hospital. Despite undergoing a series of operations, he never regained the use of his finger.

HOSPITAL

Ernie Ladd vs Johnny Powers

Cleveland, Ohio, January 1974

Bad-guy wrestlers forced to flee infuriated mob after inciting riot

Central to the wrestling villain's role is an ability to rile the audience. But Ox Baker did such an effective job of aggravating fans during a National Wrestling Federation show in 1974 that he sparked a riot.

Crowd favourite Ernie Ladd – a former American footballer – was facing arch-nemesis Johnny Powers in a bout that could only be won via submission. The match culminated with Ladd trapped in Powers' figure-four leglock. Just as he was about to escape from the manoeuvre, Baker charged into the ring, grabbed Ladd by the hair and hit him repeatedly with his trademark heart punch finisher. The move had been linked to the accidental death of wrestler Ray Gunkel in 1972, so fans didn't doubt its legitimacy.

Ladd dropped to the mat to sell the damage inflicted by the shots, at which point Baker began to stomp him. The crowd expressed its displeasure by throwing increasing amounts of litter into the ring, followed by folding chairs – one of which flew into Powers. Despite the audience being on the verge of a riot, Baker continued his assault of Ladd, serving only to further provoke the ringsiders.

Baker eventually twigged that the crowd was baying for his blood and ended his staged attack of Ladd to contend with the very real problem of how to escape from the rowdy mob. Some chair-wielding fans even clambered through the ropes in a bid to lay into the heels. After a brief face-off, Powers pelted out of the ring and through the crowd (which was now throwing bottles at him). He vaulted a barrier at the back of the arena and, closely followed by Baker, fled to the safety of the dressing room. Over 300 chairs were destroyed in the fracas, Powers and Baker both required stitches for lacerations and Ladd was sprayed with mace.

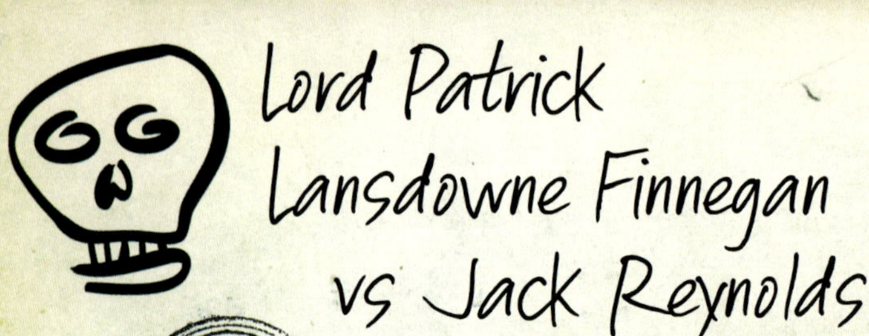

Lord Patrick Lansdowne Finnegan vs Jack Reynolds

San Francisco, California, January 1935

Enduring welterweight champion shockingly loses title to monocle-wearing aristocrat

During an era in which gimmickry in American pro wrestling was the exception rather than the rule, Jack Reynolds' no-frills approach to the 'grunt and groan game' fitted in seamlessly. A powerful amateur wrestler, he was the head wrestling coach at Indiana University. He turned pro after he was trained by Martin 'Farmer' Burns, regarded as the world's greatest grappler in the late 19th century, and was famed for his leg-split submission hold. His legitimate credentials meant that he was a perpetual holder of the world welterweight title throughout the 1920s-1930s; **The Indianapolis Star** called him a 'wonderful wrestling machine'.

But for all his professional success, he began to have difficulty in finding bookings when he was indicted by a Cincinnati grand jury in April 1934 for second-degree murder, after a man was shot and killed during a fight in a diner. He pleaded self-defence and was acquitted at the end of May - but the resultant bad publicity meant that he was relegated to working in small towns and in carnival matches after he was temporarily blacklisted by the National Wrestling Association.

In a bid to reinvigorate interest in his ailing career, he began an in-ring feud with Wilbur Finran, whose wrestling persona could not have been further removed from that of the strait-laced Reynolds. Ohio-native Finran was a pioneer of the haughty heel character and, as Lord Patrick Lansdowne Finnegan, adopted the guise of an extravagantly coiffured, monocle-wearing British nobleman who entered the ring to the accompaniment of 'God Save the King'.

Finnegan's showy antics, which included being served tea between falls by a valet, proved to be a huge draw. But despite his solid in-ring performances - he was known for his armbars, flying mares and neckbreaker finisher - this was an era in which promoters still doggedly attempted to maintain that wrestling was a legitimate sport. Titles were awarded to wrestlers who were (or, at least, could project being) stoical hard men, not to pseudo-aristocratic novelty acts.

So when Reynolds defended his welterweight title against Finnegan in January 1935, fans took it as given that the 'wrestling machine' would walk away with his championship intact - not least because he was billed as not having been defeated in 14 years. Instead, he shockingly lost the title he had been synonymous with for almost two decades (he first won it in 1917) to the self-absorbed, imitation peer of the realm.

Reynolds went on to regain the belt from Finnegan in Los Angeles 10 months later but a cultural shift had taken place: the acceptance of Finnegan proved that audiences were less concerned about the supposed integrity of the simulated sporting action than they were with being entertained by larger-than-life personalities. Such was Lord Patrick's impact, he directly influenced Gorgeous George, himself the template of the contemporary flamboyant heel.

Bruno Sammartino vs Stan Hansen

Queens, New York, June 1976

Wrestling champ saves promoter from bankruptcy by headlining show after breaking neck

It's impossible to overestimate how popular an attraction Bruno Sammartino was in the north-east United States during the 1960s-1970s. He was the archetypal hard-working yet humble babyface who was capable of fending off a seemingly endless slew of reprehensible ne'er-do-wells. His two reigns as heavyweight champion of the WWWF (the predecessor to the WWF/WWE) lasted for a total of 11 years, a record that will never be broken. Rarely has a wrestling promotion been so profoundly based around the exploits of a single man.

As such, an April 1976 Madison Square Garden main event against rookie 'Cowboy' Stan Hansen couldn't have ended more badly. Hansen attempted a bodyslam eight minutes into the contest but lost his grip and inadvertently dropped the champion on his head. Sammartino completed the match as planned before he was carted off to the hospital. 'I was told that the sixth and seventh cervical vertebrae were broken,' he says. 'I could not feel the left side of my body but I had some very good neurosurgeons and, when they were able to remove those cracked vertebrae away from the spinal cord, slowly everything started coming back.' Still, it'd be months until Sammartino would be ready to return to the ring. The WWWF couldn't afford to wait that long.

The company had booked New York's vast Shea Stadium for a show in June on which the main draw was scheduled to be a rematch between Sammartino and Hansen (whose lariat finisher, rather than the botched bodyslam, was credited as having caused his opponent's broken neck). WWWF promoter Vince McMahon Sr had made a significant investment in booking arenas around the north-east to show a live broadcast of the show along with footage of Muhammad Ali's fight against Antonio Inoki, which was taking place at the same time in Tokyo. But Inoki was unknown outside his home country and held no appeal for American wrestling fans.

'Vince McMahon started calling me at the hospital,' says Sammartino. 'He said, "Bruno, if I don't make the match between you and Stan Hansen, we could very well be going out of business." I kept saying, "How can I promise you that I'll be able to do the match when I don't know how long I'm going to be here or what kind of

shape I'll be in?" He said, "Let me at least make the match and then we'll see how you're coming along and play it by ear." Immediately all the arenas that he had committed to started selling tickets because everybody wanted to see me come back to face the guy that broke my neck. My doctors and my family were very, very angry that I agreed to it, because I was not healed enough when I went back. I was doing much better but I was by no means 100 per cent.'

A scenario was concocted that would protect Sammartino from risking further injury and give fans (32,000 turned up to Shea Stadium) the satisfaction of seeing their hero gain his revenge on Hansen. 'What we did was, when he was coming into the ring, I kicked him and all this kind of stuff,' says Sammartino. 'And he's bleeding and he went out of the ring back to the dressing room. He never laid a hand on me. And the people loved it! Absolutely went crazy. So, really, we saved the organisation.'

Gorgeous George vs Masked Marvel

Seattle, Washington, August 1952

Skirmish in middle of lake ends with flamboyant bad guy escaping in rowing boat

When the Aqua Theatre at Green Lake in Seattle was built in 1950, it was specifically designed for Seafair - a summer festival with a focus on marine events, including an attraction called the Aqua Follies, a troupe of synchronised swimmers who performed 'swimusicals'. But wrestling leagues are never slow in spotting a revenue opportunity and promoter Bob Murray realised that the quirky nature of the 5,500-seat venue would help to draw fans. Which is how Gorgeous George - the most famous wrestler of the era and one of the first stars of American television - ended up in a match that took place in a ring housed on a floating platform in the middle of the lake.

What made the spectacle even more engaging for mat fans was that George, real name George Wagner, was the archetypal flamboyant heel (both Muhammad Ali and James Brown later adopted many of his traits). George dyed his hair platinum blond and had it teased into a marcel wave - a women's haircut popular in the 1920s

achieved with heated curling irons and held in place with gold-plated pins – by Hollywood hairdressers Frank and Joseph. He wore an extravagant silk gown to the ring and was tended to by a valet who, before the match started, sprayed the ring with a perfume that George claimed was Chanel No 10. 'Why be half safe?' he would ask. All of which only served to heighten the audience's anticipation for the inevitable moment at which 'The Human Orchid' would be flung into the water.

The scrimmage began with the Marvel going on the attack and George begging off, as a lifeguard circled the ring in a small rowing boat – a device that had more to do with heightening the dramatic tension than it did with actual life-saving. The two wrestlers then fought on the narrow platform surrounding the ring before they both tumbled off it into the water, ruining George's hairdo in the process. Referee Mickey Finn attempted to haul them back into the ring, only to be dragged into the lake himself by the two combatants. 'Oh well, maybe it helps to have a name like Finn when you're making like a fish,' observed the narrator of a newsreel clip of the match.

The Masked Marvel then knocked George off the ring apron back into the water. He clambered into the lifeguard's boat, almost capsizing it in the process, before the Marvel snatched one of the oars and attempted to pummel Wagner with it. The melee culminated with Finn attempting to place the masked man in a full nelson in a bid to prevent him from clonking George with the wooden oar, only for the Marvel to hiptoss him into the lake for a final time.

George continued to appear on shows at the Aqua Theatre over the next decade. Even as late as July 1961 – just two years before his death – he lost to 'Leaping' Leo Garibaldi at the watery venue. Always keen to give the audience what they wanted, George ensured that the bout culminated with him hurling himself over the ropes and into the lake after Garibaldi hit him with a dropkick.

Lou Thesz vs Masahiro Chono

Hamamatsu, Japan, December 1990

Match ends with 74-year-old wrestler's artificial hip giving out

Aloysius Martin 'Lou' Thesz was the Cliff Richard of wrestling: he performed in seven decades, making his first appearance in the ring in 1934, his last in 1990. One of the most significant players in 20th-century American wrestling, he held the NWA world heavyweight championship for a combined total of over 10 years. His technical, if stubbornly unflashy, ring style and fearsome reputation as a 'hooker' (someone skilled in the dark art of applying excruciatingly painful submission holds) meant that promoters viewed him as the ideal figurehead for pro wrestling during an era in which it was deemed crucial to convince fans that they were watching genuine competition.

Thesz came out of retirement for one final match in December 1990, at the age of 74, to face former student Masahiro Chono in what was billed as an 'exhibition'. (Quite how this differed to any other pro wrestling match was never made clear.) With his bald pate, white vest and black spandex leggings, the veteran grappler looked like an outsize Johnny Ball gone to seed.

After Thesz escaped from a side headlock, the combatants locked fingers in a test of strength in which, ludicrously, Thesz held his own against a man almost 50 years his junior. The two combatants then gingerly exchanged old-school holds such as leg scissors, suplexes and headlock takeovers.

Ambitiously, Thesz lifted up Chono in a bid to execute a piledriver. Unfortunately for both wrestlers, Thesz's artificial hip promptly gave out. Thesz tumbled to the mat, leaving Chono dangling upside-down with his legs hooked in the ropes. On freeing himself, Chono brought the fiasco to an end by submitting his mentor with Thesz's own signature hold, the STF (a move later adopted by WWE star John Cena). Thesz, sensibly, never wrestled again.

CHAPTER 3:

BLOOD AND VIOLENCE

MUTILATION

Wahoo McDaniel vs Jimmy Garvin

Philadelphia, Pennsylvania, July 1986

Veteran bleeder loses shard of razor blade in scar tissue after slicing open own forehead

When you see a wrestler bleed, the chances are it's real blood. Contrary to the perceived wisdom that most grapplers have a joke shop's worth of blood capsules hidden down their tights, fake plasma is very rarely used in the mat game. Instead, if bloodshed is required during the course of a bout, a wrestler will hide a sliver of razor blade about their person (often in the tape wrapped around their wrists). At the required moment – for instance, after having been smacked around the head with a folding chair – the suplex specialist will fall to the mat.

While it looks as if they're clutching their head in agony, they're actually retrieving the blade and using it to slice open their forehead (a procedure known as blading). When they then stagger to their feet, it will appear as if the blow from the chair or other weapon was so powerful that it split their face open – whereas, in fact, they are suffering from a self-inflicted wound.

Wahoo McDaniel was a practised exponent of blading and frequently relied on copious bloodshed to add drama to his matches. By the mid-1980s, the veteran's heavily-scarred forehead told the grisly story of the hundreds of cuts that he had administered to himself over the previous two decades. Blading was such a frequent part of his act that when he was obliged to bleed during an Indian strap match at the *Great American Bash* against 'Gorgeous' Jimmy Garvin (a bout in which the combatants were tied to one another by a long leather leash that could be used as a weapon), he thought little of it.

At the appropriate point, McDaniel collapsed to the mat and, as he had done so many times before, reached into his wrist tape to retrieve the blade, which he then used to carve his brow open, while Garvin and his valet Precious distracted the crowd by arguing with the referee. But the old-school grappler misjudged what he was doing, cut himself too severely, and managed to lose the piece of razor blade deep in the gnarls of his disfigured brow. He was forced to wrestle the rest of the match (which he went on to win) with the blade stuck in his scalp.

It was a disgusting sight and resulted in abundant blood loss. When he returned to the dressing room, he was examined by Pennsylvania State Athletic Commission chairman James Binns, who immediately decreed that there would be no more blood on the show or at any wrestling event in the state ever again. What followed was an 18-month legal battle during which solicitors for Jim Crockett Promotions argued for wrestlers' right to bleed. The Pennsylvania House of Representatives eventually overturned the Athletic Commission's ruling and deregulated pro wrestling, leaving mat merchants in the state once again free to make use of razor blades during their routines.

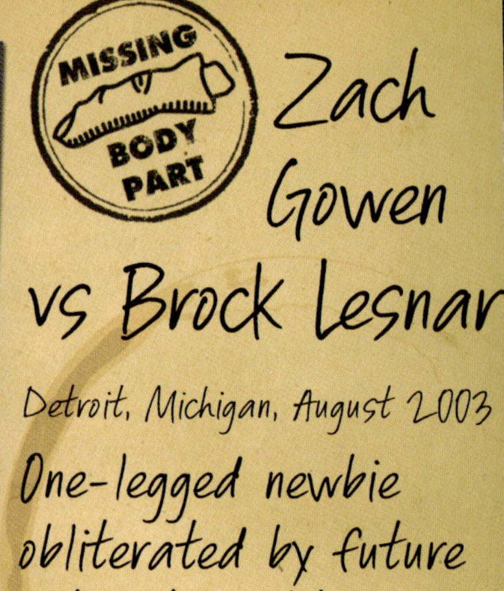

Zach Gowen vs Brock Lesnar

Detroit, Michigan, August 2003

One-legged newbie obliterated by future Ultimate Fighting champion in front of hometown crowd

When undersized, one-legged wrestler Zach Gowen was matched up in his hometown of Detroit against future UFC heavyweight champion Brock Lesnar, there was only one way it could go: Gowen was in for one of the most convincing beatings in modern wrestling history.

Gowen's left leg was removed when he was eight, as a result of osteogenic sarcoma, a cancer that could have been fatal had it spread. By the summer of 2003 - little over a year after his pro debut - he was in the midst of a short-lived stint in WWE, during which he played a plucky underdog. 'One week I'm bagging groceries and the next week I'm on TV with Vince McMahon, Hulk Hogan and Roddy Piper,' he says. Lesnar, meanwhile, was wholly credible in his role of the huge, unforgiving bully. 'He was like something out of a videogame,' notes Gowen.

BLOOD

Before the bell rang to signify the start of the contest, Lesnar casually left the ring to taunt Gowen's mother, who was sitting in the front row. A hopping mad Gowen took the opportunity to vault over the top rope on to a distracted Lesnar, which – in an inspired move – he followed by clubbing him with the prosthetic leg that he had removed prior to the match. It was the last offence the 20-year-old would have all night. Lesnar was soon disqualified when he clouted the one-legged wonder in the head with a folding chair but the onslaught continued as he flung Gowen – who had bladed and was, by now, bleeding extravagantly – leg-first into the ring post. Twice. As a finishing touch, Lesnar tipped Gowen off the stretcher that he was being wheeled away on.

It was, says Gowen, 'one of the easiest, funnest matches I've ever had because I didn't have to do anything. All I had to do was get beat up, which is what I'm good at. For Brock to destroy the hometown kid in front of his family was really good TV. Brock was a real nice guy – he really took care of me. That's where the magic of pro wrestling is: to make it look like he's killing me but he's not really hurting me at all.'

In fact, the only real damage was to Lesnar – and that was before the match even started. Prior to the show, Lesnar, Gowen and WWE boss Vince McMahon were in the ring, discussing what would happen during the bout. 'The original plan was that I would try to dive on to Brock but he would catch me and ram me into the post,' explains Gowen. 'Vince goes, "Well, that's a great idea. Why don't you guys try it?" And so I dove over the top rope but I came in a little too high and, on the way down, my right hip clipped him in the jaw. And it knocked him clean out. I think Brock was a little embarrassed but it was totally my fault. I don't know if I'm the only person to ever knock him out, either accidentally or on purpose, but I can say that I knocked out Brock Lesnar, UFC heavyweight champion.'

Raven vs Shane Douglas

Nashville, Tennessee, September 2003

Chaotic main event results in one wrestler vomiting mid-match and another receiving an accidental scalping

It was a simple plan, one that honoured a proven, if time-worn, wrestling tradition. The hostility between Scott 'Raven' Levy and 'The Franchise' Shane Douglas would finally be resolved by a showdown in which the loser would suffer the ignominy of having their head shaved bald. It's a stipulation that dates back to the 1940s and one that has remained popular thanks to its delivery of a palpable resolution to a dispute and the perceived humiliation suffered by the loser. After a hard-fought struggle littered with outside interference and unconscious referees, Douglas would finally better his nemesis and take his hair as a trophy. Which is what happened – albeit with a couple of unanticipated incidents along the way.

Douglas was addicted to prescription painkillers at the time and was bloated and out of shape. With less than 10 minutes on the clock, he was completely winded and struggling to continue with the match. He managed to hiptoss Raven over the top rope to the floor and then staggered out of the ring after him, mouth agape. He rolled Levy back into the squared circle and, as he followed him through the ropes, vomited profusely, just missing his unfortunate opponent's head.

In an attempt to recover, he knelt down next to the ropes with a knee across Raven's throat, before standing back up. As he did so, he immediately doubled over and spat more bile to the canvas. Levy attempted to maintain the flow of the match and hit 'The Franchise' with a pair of faux punches and a knee to the face, after which Douglas crumpled to the mat – not because of the staged violence but due to the very real disaster that was taking place in his stomach. He threw up once again, this time directly in front of the camera, leaving a large pool of sick on the mat.

Gamely, Raven continued to do his best to maintain the facade that they were locked in combat, and attempted to pin Douglas, who grabbed the ropes to force a break. Douglas then shifted to his left, narrowly avoiding rolling into his own puke. Suitably purged, he went on to win the match as planned. But the evening's mishaps didn't end there. The stipulations now dictated that, having lost the match, Raven would have his head shaved. Resigned to his fate, he sat on a folding chair in the middle of the ring as Douglas's manager James Mitchell went to work with the clippers provided by the promotion, TNA. The idea was to give the defeated wrestler a number one haircut – instead, he received an excruciating mauling.

The clippers that had been obtained were, in fact, designed to shear sheep and had exceptionally sharp teeth. While using the device, Mitchell was also inadvertently holding it upside down. As a result, in addition to removing Raven's hair in a single swipe, the tool was also tearing into his scalp, leaving the top of his head a mauled, bloody mess on which gaping wounds were abundantly evident to both ringside fans and viewers at home. Once backstage, Mitchell apologised profusely but was convinced that he was in for a genuine beating for the gruesome mishap. Raven did swing at him but thought better of it at the last moment and instead just wiped the blood off his head and into Mitchell's face. Mitchell later confessed that he thought the unplanned scalping 'made for great TV'.

Cactus Jack vs Sandman Philadelphia, Pennsylvania, February 1995

Concussed wrestler forgets that he's supposed to lose Texas Death Match

HOSPITAL

INJURY

The original incarnation of Extreme Championship Wrestling did wonders for kitchenware sales in the Philadelphia area in the mid-1990s. Fans were encouraged to attend shows equipped with objects that wrestlers could grab off them mid-match and use as weapons. Frying pans proved to be a particularly popular choice: rarely would an event take place at the self-styled ECW Arena (actually a dilapidated warehouse in one of the less salubrious areas of south Philly) without at least one performer receiving a frighteningly stiff head shot with said utensil.

So it was little surprise that a pan came into play when noted brawlers Mick 'Cactus Jack' Foley and Jim 'Sandman' Fullington met in a Texas Death Match, which could only be won by knocking down your opponent for a count of 10. Just two minutes into the scrap, Cactus grabbed a skillet from the crowd and smashed it over Sandman's cranium with such brain-rattling force that it gave him a concussion.

Fullington spent the rest of the match in a complete daze: he had no idea what he was meant to do and, much of the time, could barely stand up. Foley was, in effect, forced to have a bout with himself (missing elbow drops seemed to be the key to doing this effectively). After a few minutes of shoddy action, Foley took Sandman outside the ring, violently flung a chair at his head and then drove him face-first to the concrete floor with a DDT, for what was intended to have been the match-winning 10-count.

Sandman, however, genuinely forgot that he was meant to stay put and insisted on sitting up. Cactus was forced to perform another two DDTs on his brain-injured opponent, after which Fullington finally conceded defeat. He was then whisked to hospital and sidelined for two weeks.

Jimmy Snuka vs Lou Albano

New York, November 1982

Cyndi Lauper's on-screen father goes to ring drunk before shamelessly hacking open own forehead

Along with Bobby 'The Brain' Heenan, Captain Lou Albano (not actually a real captain) was one of the WWF's great managers – a charismatic mouthpiece for a villainous parade of tag teams. But he demonstrated far less prowess on the rare occasions in the early 1980s when he put aside his managerial role and stepped into the ring himself. The nadir was a 1982 contest with Jimmy 'Superfly' Snuka.

Albano entered the squared circle clad in trainers, jogging bottoms and an unbuttoned Hawaiian shirt that exposed his flabby belly. An enthusiastic boozer, he was also drunk. This, combined with his complete lack of athletic ability, meant that Snuka didn't have a hope of extracting a plausible match from the Captain. Indeed, Albano barely responded to Snuka's blows, even when the 'Superfly' first delivered one his supposedly devastating headbutts, a move that would leave other wrestlers writhing in faux agony.

Instead, Albano – who played the role of Cyndi Lauper's father in the video for 1983 hit single 'Girls Just Want to Have Fun' – wandered around the ring looking mildly irritated. As the chaotic match plodded on, Snuka continued to punch the inebriated Albano, who then openly reached into his right pocket. Albano strolled to the opposite side of the ring and, while looking directly into the TV camera, used the craft knife that he'd just retrieved to slice himself across the forehead, in an incompetent bid to give the impression that Snuka's pulled punches had, in fact, split his face open.

Snuka followed up with yet more thumps to the head of his bungling foe, while Albano staggered around the ring attempting to tag in a partner who didn't exist. With proceedings all-but falling apart, the referee called off the contest and awarded the match to Snuka (Albano refused to lose by pinfall), mercifully ending one of the most woefully amateurish matches the WWF ever promoted.

Hulk Hogan vs Harley Race

Nashville, Tennessee, March 1988

Former world champion almost dies after dive through table goes awry

'Watcha gonna do when Hulkamania runs wild on you?!' This was the oft-repeated refrain burned into the frontal lobe of anyone who watched WWF programming in the 1980s. Despite his curious appearance - bleached blond handlebar moustache, Terry Nutkins bald patch/mullet combo, and a skin tone that suggested an accident with a sunbed - Hulk Hogan was the decade's most popular wrestler, Hulkamania the WWF's leading money-spinner. To maintain his position as the ultimate wrestling icon, Hogan was fed an extensive parade of villains. Typically, they were ugly do-badders such as King Kong Bundy and Andre the Giant, who would use their enormous size to bully the heroic 'Hulkster'.

In between the formulaic confrontations with barely-mobile leviathans, Hogan was occasionally matched with opponents who had greater ambitions for their matches than simply exchanging punches. One such adversary was Harley Race, an eight-time former NWA champion known for his rugged ring style, who faced Hogan during a taping for an episode of *Saturday Night's Main Event* in March 1988.

Near the end of the match, Race set up Hogan on a table at ringside (this was a decade before such furniture-based shenanigans became a regular part of WWF routines). The veteran grappler then performed his trademark diving headbutt off the ring apron, while the 'Hulkster', predictably enough, moved out of the way. The table had far less give than Race had anticipated and, after he crashed through it awkwardly, he was left in severe pain. Nonetheless, the match continued as planned and Hogan went on to pin Race following his usual legdrop finisher.

'Generally, if I was going to do anything like that, I'd walk out there before the match and see what I was actually going to have to land on,' says Race. 'And this particular night I didn't bother to do it. It got me.' Indeed, Race was left with a ruptured intestine (he later had 18 inches of it removed), a bacterial infection and peritonitis, an extremely painful inflammation of the membrane that lines the abdomen. Remarkably, there was no indication that Race was so severely injured: he just carried on with the contest. 'I knew I was hurt at the time,' he admits. 'But, as far as the pain, when your adrenaline is pumping like that, you really don't notice that until after you've quit what you're doing and given it a chance to catch up with you.'

Despite the physical discomfort that Race was in, he continued to honour his wrestling bookings for the next few weeks. 'After *WrestleMania IV* [which took place three weeks later], I flew back home to Kansas City. When I woke up the following morning, I immediately had a rush of pain and blacked out. When I came to from that, I just called the hospital and they came and picked me up. They didn't know if I was going to live or die.' Against the advice of his doctors, Race returned to the ring seven months later, while in the midst of a bitter divorce. 'I was going through so much crap at that point in time that returning to wrestling was one way of getting away from it.'

Henri Deglane vs Ed Lewis

Montreal, Canada, May 1931

Fearsome hardman cheated out of heavyweight title when opponent gnaws on own arm

When Ed 'Strangler' Lewis defended his American Wrestling Association world heavyweight championship against Henri Deglane in May 1931, he had been champion for only three weeks. His title reign began when he beat Ed Don George for the strap in Los Angeles. George was originally supposed to retain the championship against Lewis but, as the match began, Lewis nonchalantly informed the champion during the introductions that he was going to leave the ring with the title and that they could either do it the easy way or the hard way. George knew that he could never beat the fearsome Lewis in a legitimate contest and, sensibly, opted for the easy way and gave Lewis the victory.

With his hardman reputation, Lewis had little concern that an opponent would attempt to employ a similar tactic with him. But the crafty Deglane - who won a gold medal in Greco-Roman wrestling at the 1924 Olympics and, according to **Wrestling World** magazine, had 'thick muscles developed by carrying barrels of wine in a Parisian winery' - came up with another scheme, in conjunction with promoter Paul Bowser, to prise the championship from the 'Strangler'.

Lewis entered the ring having been told that he would retain his title by beating Deglane two falls to one. At the time, wrestlers returned to the dressing room between falls, while an intermission took place. As per the script, Lewis allowed Deglane to take the first fall in 33 minutes, expecting to then win the two remaining falls and retain the belt. But during the interval prior to the second session, Deglane viciously bit his own arm until it started to bleed. Back in the ring, he covered the wound until he suddenly started to hysterically scream, 'He bit me!'

DOUBLE CROSS

The 'Strangler' had no idea what was going on and backed away from his shrieking opponent. Referee Eugene Tremblay (himself a former lightweight wrestler) saw the blood and the marks on Deglane's arm and assumed that Lewis had sunk his teeth into his adversary. Even though it was not the planned finish, the ref had no choice but to disqualify Lewis and award the championship to Deglane.

Lewis's manager Billy Sandow demanded that a photographer should take pictures of Deglane's wounds while he was still in the ring, to prove that the teeth marks were, in fact, his own. But the referee would hear nothing of the protestations that Lewis had been double-crossed and the title change stood, as Deglane continued to howl with pain. A furious Lewis stormed backstage in a bid to pummel the conniving Bowser. But the promoter was prepared for such an eventuality and had surrounded himself with six baseball bat-wielding bodyguards. As a result of the match, most wrestling promotions in North America subsequently decreed that championships could not change hands on a disqualification - a ruling that is still employed by WWE today.

Deglane held the title for the Boston-based AWA for almost two years, until he lost it back to Ed Don George in February 1933 in a match in which he suffered a broken collarbone. He later returned to his native France, where he remained the country's top pro wrestling star until well into the 1950s.

Ed "Strangler" Lewis

British Bulldogs vs Hart Foundation

Tampa, Florida, January 1987

Tag champ ordered to appear in match despite inability to walk

When Davey Boy Smith and Tom 'Dynamite Kid' Billington – collectively known as the British Bulldogs – faced Don Muraco and Bob Orton Jr at an event in Hamilton, Canada on 13 December 1986, the duo expected to have a routine defence of their WWF tag team championship. Instead, it was the night that the cumulative effect of the years of abuse taken by Dynamite's back (he was famed for his spectacular, stunt-filled matches) finally caught up with him.

He felt a twinge in his back before the bout but thought nothing more of it. During the match, while running the ropes, he felt something go in his back and crumpled to the mat in agony. He slowly rolled towards his corner to tag in his partner and Smith completed the match while Billington lay on the ring apron, until he was stretchered backstage and then taken by ambulance to hospital.

He was diagnosed with two ruptured discs in his back and underwent a six-hour operation to have them removed. Three specialists instructed him to retire from wrestling. He ignored them and discharged himself from hospital. While still recovering at home, he was pressurised into returning to the ring by WWF owner Vince McMahon – despite the fact that he could barely walk. The company's television shows were taped weeks in advance, so viewers had no idea that Billington was injured: even after having surgery, Dynamite continued to appear on television with Smith defending the tag titles. At non-televised shows, Davey Boy teamed with a variety of stand-in tag partners.

But for the sake of continuity, McMahon insisted that Dynamite returned for a one-off match at a television taping on 26 January 1987 in order to drop the belts to the Hart Foundation team of Bret 'Hitman' Hart and Jim 'The Anvil' Neidhart. Billington's appearance shocked his fellow wrestlers when they saw him backstage: he was using a wheelchair and, without his usual diet of steroids and workouts, he had lost 50lbs. He struggled into his ring gear, which now hung off him loosely, and had to walk arm-in-arm with Smith in order to make it down the aisle.

Dynamite was in no condition to even clamber into the ring, let alone wrestle a match, so a simple ruse was employed to excuse him from duty. During the Bulldogs' entrance, Bret Hart ran up behind him and, using the loud hailer that was habitually carried by his manager Jimmy Hart (no relation), gently knocked Billington to the floor, where he remained for the entirety of the match, clutching his head.

Smith briefly held his own against the nefarious Hart Foundation but, after just three minutes of action, the villains executed their Hart Attack running clothesline finisher and 'The Anvil' pinned him to secure the tag team gold. The bout was broadcast two weeks later and viewers were given no indication of the real reason the Bulldogs had to lose the titles. Although he left the WWF in November 1988, Dynamite didn't have his final match until October 1996. His ring injuries later left him paralysed from the waist down.

D-Von Dudley & Mass Transit vs The Gangstas

Revere, Massachusetts, November 1996

Ex-bounty hunter charged with assault after slicing open rookie's face with scalpel during match

BLOOD

Eric Kulas's first (and last) match for ECW didn't go particularly well. The 17-year-old dreamed of securing regular work with the blood and weapons-fuelled promotion and turned up on spec at a local show to ask if he could appear on the undercard. He had previously wrestled on a dozen or so low-rent independent shows, on which he would face his trainer, a midget wrestler who used the nom de plume Tiny the Terrible. He hoped to repeat his shtick with Tiny in Revere but, when ECW regular Axl Rotten failed to turn up as expected, he was used as a last-minute replacement in a tag match in which he would team with D-Von Dudley against The Gangstas, New Jack and Mustafa Saed.

The 350-pound Kulas was to play the role of an overweight bus driver named Mass Transit. As was de rigueur for matches involving The Gangstas, he was required to bleed after being hit with a selection of inanimate objects and, before the bout took place, Kulas agreed that he would allow New Jack – a former bounty hunter who had killed four men – to cut him across the forehead. But the subsequent violence inflicted on the rookie far exceeded anything that usually took place within the guise of pro wrestling.

The Gangstas charged into the ring carrying dustbins full of household objects, which they would use as weapons. Dudley spent the majority of the match outside the ring, while his impromptu tag partner was assaulted inside the squared circle. New Jack broke a wooden crutch over Kulas's skull and drilled him in the face with a metal toaster, causing the huge rookie to collapse to the mat. As Kulas sat back up, New Jack stood behind him, grabbed his chin and sliced him methodically across the forehead with a scalpel. Kulas screamed and fell to the canvas, clutching his face. When he raised his head, the horrific nature of the wound became immediately apparent: not only was his face awash with blood, he was bleeding with such force that it left a large, dark red puddle on the mat.

As his father at ringside screamed, 'That's enough! Ring the fucking bell – he's 17!' (Kulas had told the promotion he was 19), New Jack and Mustafa continued to smack him across the face with objects. Mustafa executed an awkward-looking bodyslam on his teenage opponent (who, oddly, seemed to be primarily concerned with pulling his trousers up at this point), before New Jack dove off the top rope with a chair, which landed with full force across Kulas's face.

The Gangsta pinned his battered foe but there was no referee to count the fall – curiously, the entire bout had taken place without an official. Kulas lay in the ring with blood continuing to pour from his brow and the beating finally ended when a medic crawled into the ring to attend to the wannabe wrestler. Such was the extent of Kulas's blood loss, the first aider ran out of the towels she was using to stem the flow and had to resort to pressing T-shirts against Kulas's forehead. The defeated grappler was eventually stretchered off (he required 50 stitches to sew his face back together) and the show was halted for 25 minutes while the ring crew mopped up the blood.

New Jack, who was notorious for dishing out violent reprisals against wrestlers he perceived to have slighted him, was later charged with aggravated assault and assault with a deadly weapon but was cleared on both counts after Kulas proved to be a wholly unreliable witness. The grappling hopeful never achieved his ambition of becoming an eminent wrestler and died at the age of 22 due to complications related to his obesity.

Manny Fernandez vs Invader III

Cataño, Puerto Rico, December 1988

Masked man feigns injury by projectile vomiting blood across ring

What Puerto Rico's World Wrestling Council lacked in mainstream stars it often attempted to compensate for with copious amounts of bloodshed and carnage (it pioneered the use of barbed wire and fire long before they became staples of 1990s hardcore wrestling). Such tactics were never more apparent than during this gruesome spectacle between 'Raging Bull' Manny Fernandez and the mask-wearing Invader III (Johnny Rivera).

After five minutes of rudimentary exchanges, which largely consisted of Invader slapping on a side headlock, the masked man missed a dive from the middle turnbuckle. This was the cue for Fernandez to hit a kneedrop off the top rope, which the commentators claimed broke Invader's sternum.

As Invader writhed on the mat, the 'Raging Bull' connected with another pair of top-rope kneedrops, causing his felled opponent to spew fountains of blood. Within seconds, Invader's entire mask, upper body and half the mat were swathed in claret. The referee frantically called for the bell, while fellow wrestlers swarmed from the backstage area to offer assistance.

In an era in which wrestling storylines were often so spurious that it was almost impossible for viewers to suspend their disbelief, seeing someone projectile vomit blood across the ring gave the appearance that genuine hostilities had taken place. Despite this, the grisly stunt has rarely been repeated, perhaps due to the fact that Invader apparently achieved the effect by ingesting pig's blood and vodka before the match, which he then regurgitated at the required moment.

BLOOD

Antonio Inoki vs Hulk Hogan

Tokyo, Japan, June 1983

'Hulkster' tournament victory part of hoax that fools fans for two decades

When New Japan Pro Wrestling's Antonio Inoki faced Hulk Hogan in the final of a tournament dubbed the International Wrestling Grand Prix, it was fully expected that Inoki would win. He was long-established as the company's premier attraction and, as such, rarely lost.

The actual result took everyone by surprise – and fooled both fans and wrestlers for almost 20 years. As Inoki clambered on to the ring apron after both men had tumbled over the top rope to the floor, Hogan hit him with his Japanese finisher, the Axe Bomber (essentially nothing more than a running clothesline). Inoki plummeted back to the ringside area, while the referee began his count and Hogan gloated in the ring.

Within seconds, though, it appeared as if something was seriously amiss and a slew of officials and other wrestlers crowded around the prone fighter. Inoki was apparently unconscious after swallowing his tongue, leaving the referee no choice but to halt the match and award the tournament to Hogan – which onlookers thought was an impromptu, and legitimate, finish to a bout that his Japanese opponent had been scheduled to win. Inoki was eventually hauled back into the ring and tended to by a doctor, as distraught fans chanted his name.

But the match had gone exactly as planned: Inoki hadn't really swallowed his tongue and it was simply a ruse to generate interest in a rematch with the 'Hulkster'. For years, both parties insisted otherwise and the pretence was only blown after the publication in 2001 of a tell-all book written by former New Japan referee Pete Takahashi.

As the leading draw of the weekly shows at Memphis's Mid-South Coliseum throughout the 1970s and 1980s, Jerry 'The King' Lawler faced a succession of wily villains. One of his most famous - and certainly most unlikely - opponents was Andy Kaufman, part avant-garde comedian, part performance artist.

Kaufman had been a fan of pro wrestling since his childhood, when his grandmother would take him to New York's Madison Square Garden to watch wrestlers such as Bruno Sammartino and arrogant baddie 'Nature Boy' Buddy Rogers, whom he idolised. He integrated his love of wrestling into his performances at comedy clubs, during which he challenged female members of the audience to grappling contests. He subsequently crowned himself the world intergender wrestling champion and offered $1,000 and his hand in marriage to any woman who could pin his shoulders to the mat.

Eager to extend his involvement in the grap game, he approached then-WWF boss Vince McMahon Sr, pitching a storyline that would bring him into the promotion and afford him the opportunity to wrestle at the Garden. McMahon wasn't convinced that Kaufman's act was right for his territory, which was built around huge, sinister-looking heels vying for the WWF title. So the comedian instead took his proposal to the more receptive Tennessee-based Continental Wrestling Association where, in late 1981 - having adopted an outrageously misogynistic persona - he began wrestling women on shows at the Mid-South Coliseum.

Jerry Lawler vs Andy Kaufman

Memphis, Tennessee, April 1982

Sitcom star faces local wrestling hero... and ends up in traction

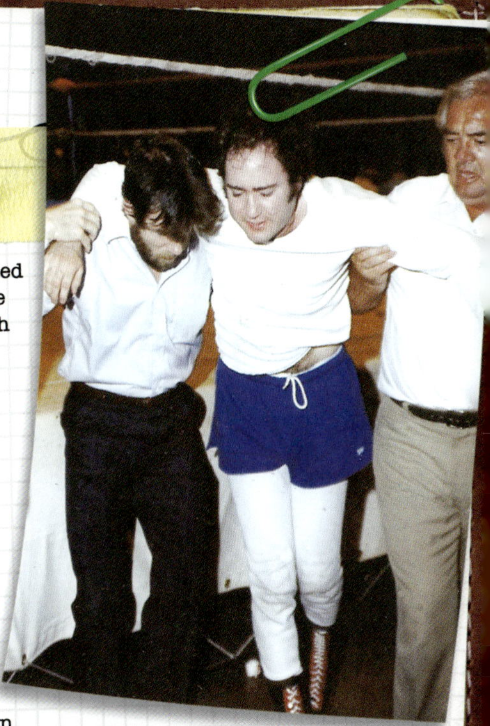

As the comedian's undefeated streak lengthened, the narrative arced towards a showdown with Jerry Lawler, which would be Kaufman's first bout against another man. The scrawny TV star (he played a mechanic in highly-rated sitcom *Taxi* from 1978-1983) couldn't have looked less like a wrestler, thanks to the combination of his slight build and ring attire that consisted of a pair of shorts atop white thermal underwear.

Kaufman was living out his fantasy of playing a wrestling bad guy and, with an intrinsic knack for trash-talking and manipulating the audience, was incredibly effective in the role for someone who hadn't spent years learning the craft. What he wasn't, though, was a plausible opponent for local hero Lawler. Kaufman began the bout, which took place in front of 8,000 baying fans, by stalling and refusing to lock up with 'The King', eventually prompting Lawler to grab the microphone and ask, 'Have you come down here to wrestle or act like an ass?' After five minutes of non-action, Lawler stood in the centre of the ring, placed his hands behind his back and leaned forwards in order to give Kaufman a free shot.

The comedian finally placed Lawler in a feeble-looking side headlock, which Lawler reversed into a high back suplex – one that inadvertently landed Kaufman on his head. 'The King' followed up with a piledriver, an illegal move under Memphis rules, for which he was disqualified. After taking a second piledriver, Kaufman was whisked off to St Francis Hospital. The plan had always been that the actor would come out of the match unscathed but would purport to have suffered a serious injury. In practice, although the damage wasn't as severe as he portrayed (he wore a brace in public for months), he really did strain his neck and was in traction for the next three days.

Cactus Jack vs Big Van Vader

Munich, Germany, March 1994

Wrestler's ear ripped off after reckless stunt goes appallingly wrong

Big Van Vader was known for his hard-hitting wrestling style: his approach to making the grap game look legitimate was largely based around the notion of giving his opponents a genuine beating. But the most gruesome injury sustained by one of his adversaries had more to do with the ring crew than it did with his own brutal offence.

In March 1994, US-based league WCW was on a tour of Germany, where it had garnered a loyal following thanks to its TV slot on sports channel DSF. After one of the preliminary scraps on a show in Munich, Too Cold Scorpio - a high-flying wrestler who used the tension of the ring ropes as a springboard for his spectacular aerial manoeuvres - complained that the ropes were too loose. WCW had hired local stage hands who were unfamiliar with the American ring and, in response to Scorpio's grievance, simply tightened the ropes to their maximum tension.

Future WWF champion Mick Foley (then wrestling as Cactus Jack) was in the midst of a violent feud with Vader at the time: Foley would usually be in pain for a few days after each of their matches but dismissed it as the price he had to pay for having some of the best WCW matches of the era. But on this particular night, Vader was suffering an injury of his own and had lost the feeling in his fingers. Foley agreed to work around it, performing stunts that would still make Vader appear to be an unstoppable monster. After about seven minutes of action, Foley knocked Vader out of the ring.

As Vader clambered back into the squared circle, Foley charged straight at him. Vader ducked out of the way and Foley flew head first into the ropes and performed one of his trademark sequences.

Foley landed in such a way that his head became trapped between the top two ropes, which were now entangled. The idea was that the grappler carrying out the move was hung by the neck for a few seconds, legs flailing, before flipping back into the ring with the aid of the referee. It wasn't an easy move to perform and WCW rings made it all the more difficult as the ring ropes were actually lift cables wrapped in rubber casing. But it produced a dramatic effect and was a frequent component of the Cactus Jack repertoire.

Except this time, thanks to the cables having been fully tightened, Foley was legitimately trapped. Realising that the performance had become all too real, he panicked and screamed for help. His only means of escape was to prise the ropes apart with the aid of the ref. But the ropes were wound so tightly that he was unable to create a large enough gap and, in the process of falling to the floor, Foley's right ear was sliced off.

As he lay on the ground, there was little indication that this was anything other than part of the act. Indeed, after a few moments he clambered back into the ring and continued with the match. Observant ringsiders would have then noticed the referee pick something up off the mat: Foley's ear. The ref handed it to the ring announcer, who raced backstage to place it in an ice-filled plastic bag. At no point did anyone, least of all Foley, consider bringing the match to an impromptu halt due to the very real injury that he had sustained. He went ahead with the match's final few sequences before succumbing to defeat, as arranged, following a clothesline.

After the bout, Foley was carted off to a nearby hospital for an emergency operation. The surgeon was unable to reattach the ear as so many cells had been destroyed and instead placed the missing ear's cartilage in an artificial pocket above the remaining lobe. A nurse then dropped the remains of Foley's severed appendage in the bin. He returned to the ring a month later.

Mitch Page vs Mad Man Pondo

Charlestown, Indiana, June 2000

Weapons match abandoned after wrestler accidentally slices off half of opponent's face

BLOOD

COCK UP

MUTILATION

The lot of the hardcore wrestler on the US indie scene is a thankless one, consisting as it does of being mutilated with a bizarre array of inanimate objects in front of small crowds for modest pay-offs. The best you can hope for is to be able to walk away with only relatively superficial injuries – something that Mitch Page resolutely failed to do following a weapons match with Mad Man Pondo.

Less than two minutes into the violent showdown, Pondo smashed a large wooden clock, face first, over Page's head, which elicited an 'Ooooo!' from the crowd and a smattering of applause. Page slumped forward and the referee leant in to inspect the damage. He was horrified by what he saw: the entire right-hand side of Page's face was awash with blood and a huge piece of skin and flesh flapped hideously over his ear.

The match was abandoned immediately – the bell wasn't even rung as the referee raced to the side of the ring and yelled, 'We need help!' Ringsiders quickly realised the gravity of the situation and also began to scream 'EMTs!' as a fan frantically dialled for an ambulance from her mobile phone. Page somehow got to his feet and staggered towards the ropes, before he collapsed in the corner.

Pondo rushed over to help and tried to reassure him, while pressing a towel to his face in a bid to stem the blood loss. The gruesome wound later required over 100 stitches to close it. Not to be dissuaded by the incident, Page returned to action less than three months later to compete in a 'Caribbean spider net glass deatmatch'.

CHAPTER 4:

BIZARRE SETTINGS

Matt & Nick Jackson vs Don Fujii & Masaaki Mochizuki Tokyo, Japan, August 2008

Mat merchants forced to wrestle on floor after new ring disintegrates

Seeing the ring collapse after the first match is never a good way to begin an evening of professional wrestling. Which was exactly what happened at an event promoted by Dragon Gate, a Japanese outfit that specialises in high-flying contests between lighter-weight grapplers. Japanese rings are traditionally harder and less forgiving than American versions, so the company decided to invest in a model imported from California. This was the first time it had been used.

'We were watching the first match backstage on the monitor,' says American wrestler Matt Jackson, who was scheduled to have a tag team match later that night with brother Nick. 'Someone took a bump and then the ring just imploded.

They got through the match but the ring was destroyed.'
In a vain attempt to resolve the problem, the referee tried to straighten out one of the ring posts by kicking it as hard as he could - with the result that the entire structure caved in. 'One side of the ring fell off completely,' laughs Jackson. 'There was no way we could keep wrestling on this thing.'

Most promotions would have decided to cancel the six remaining matches but Dragon Gate decided that the show must go on, ring or otherwise. What remained of the ring was taken down and its wooden boards and padding were taped to the floor. The rest of the card would take place on this makeshift crash mat, even if it meant that much of the planned action had to be ditched. 'We actually had an entire match all planned out,' says Jackson. 'Once we found out we were wrestling on the floor, we had to pretty much scrap it all. But it was much easier than people might have expected because we turned it into more of a brawl.'

Hence the Jacksons dominated the start of the match with their tandem offence, until all four fought into the stands. The heel team executed a double piledriver on Matt on the concrete floor, which laid him out for the next few minutes. This allowed Fujii and Mochizuki to victimise younger brother Nick, who adopted the guise of hero in peril. 'They were just dismantling Nick with their kicks and strikes,' says Matt. 'He was sore for about a week after that. Then I finally made a big comeback and we got a sneak roll-up out of nowhere.'

Although the match had been amended to accommodate the fact that there was no ring, the wrestlers still found it disconcerting to be fighting with neither ropes nor turnbuckles. 'It was a very strange night,' says the elder Jackson. 'We had some fun with it though. During some spots, we would act like we were going to go hit the ropes and that we'd forgotten they weren't there, so the crowd really liked that.'

The trashed ring was never used again. 'I know that they were really upset with this guy from Anaheim who built this really crappy ring for them,' says Jackson. 'After that, they ended up going back to the old Japanese one.'

Blacktop Bully vs Dustin Rhodes

Atlanta, Georgia, March 1995

Over-enthusiastic grapple merchants fired following brawl on back of lorry

If ever a concept was doomed to failure, surely it was WCW's King of the Road match. The idea was that, instead of fighting within the confines of a traditional ring, the protagonists would face one another in a cage that was on the back of a moving 18-wheel truck. Rather than victory being achieved via the usual pinfall or submission, it was possible to win only by pulling an air horn, situated at the front of the enclosure.

The parameters of the bout meant that Blacktop Bully (previously Smash in WWF tag team Demolition) and Dustin Rhodes (better known as Goldust) were never going to have a quality encounter. The wrestlers were also under strict instructions to adhere to WCW's 'no blood' policy of the time: a rule they flagrantly ignored by nicking themselves with hidden shards of razor blade. The two grapplers were later fired for their insubordination.

The scrap was taped on the outskirts of Atlanta, Georgia but broadcast as if it was taking place live as part of a pay-per-view event in Tupelo, Mississippi five days later. Due to the unsanctioned blood loss, seven minutes was cut from the match (which was won by Blacktop). Of the remaining footage that did air, much of it consisted of distant overhead shots from a helicopter, in order to disguise the degree of violence that had taken place. The end result was a match that was edited so comprehensively it was rendered entirely incoherent. And the name of the show it was part of? *WCW Uncensored.*

Killer Bees vs Mike Sharpe & Barry O

San Juan, Puerto Rico, October 1985

Luckless wrestlers vainly attempt to perform match in middle of rainstorm

When a torrential downpour hit San Juan in the midst of an open-air WWF show, the promotion simply decided to ignore the weather and carry on with the event. The result was a series of matches that were held in hilariously inhospitable conditions. The participants in this tag bout were soaked before the opening bell even rang and the waterlogged ring meant they were only able to perform the most rudimentary wrestling manoeuvres or risk slipping over.

To begin with, the combatants did nothing more than exchange armlocks, as the remaining fans at ringside - by this point, there were no more than a few hundred spectators left in a stadium that could house up to 19,000 people - attempted to shelter under umbrellas and, ambitiously, folding wooden chairs.

Meanwhile, the Killer Bees' Jim Brunzell threw Sharpe into the ropes and hit him with an elbow, which caused Sharpe to fall to the mat, where he landed in a pool of water. Barry O (the uncle of future WWE champion Randy Orton) then tagged in and appeared determined to attempt more elaborate holds but could only manage a snapmare takeover. Brunzell retaliated with a snapmare of his own, while it started raining sideways.

Barry O was then only saved from slipping over as Brunzell held him up by the hair. Referee Danny Davis was less fortunate and performed a spectacular, if unintentional, pratfall, the highlight of the entire shambolic contest.
After a barely coherent tussle that lasted a total of just four minutes, Brunzell cradled Barry O for the match-ending three-count. In a puddle.

Chaz Taylor vs Steven Dane

Dallas, Texas, August 1992

Wrestler wins match by forcing opponent to take bungee jump

SURREAL

Wrestling feuds traditionally culminate with some form of novelty match, whether it be in a cage or under submission rules. For the feud between Chaz Taylor and Steve Dane, the short-lived Global Wrestling Federation chose to come up with a gimmick all of its own: the bungee match. A crane was positioned outside of the promotion's home venue, the Dallas Sportatorium, at the end of which was a small cage that was open on one side. The two wrestlers were strapped to bungee cords before they clambered into the enclosure, which was then raised to – according to the announcers, at least – a height of 190ft. To win the showdown, you had to force your opponent to plummet out of the cage.

Once the crane began to reel in its load, it was difficult to tell what was going on as the match was filmed solely from the ground – there was no camera on the bungee platform itself. Viewers were treated to a view of the underside of the pen, from which Taylor's legs protruded, while Dane supposedly laid into him with a series of kicks. Brilliantly, the announcers – who were standing below the crane – were forced to commentate on a match they couldn't see.

Taylor teased that he was about to topple off the ledge until he grabbed Dane and flung him over his head into the darkness of the Texas night. Dane flapped about uselessly in mid-air as the crane lowered him back to earth. The entire debacle was over in less than three minutes. With both wrestlers back on terra firma, Taylor's mother rushed over to hug him. The victorious fighter then exclaimed, 'I saw my life flash between my eyes. I saw the ground in 3D! I need not say no more.' Indeed, he need not.

Atsushi Onita, Mr Gannosuke & Katsutoshi Niiyama vs Mr Pogo, The Gladiator & Hideki Hosaka

Tokyo, Japan, September 1994

Bonkers promoter devises match that takes place in exploding swimming pool

During its early-1990s heyday, Japan's Frontier Martial-Arts Wrestling was home to some of the most outlandish wrestling bouts ever conceived, which would invariably involve top star (and owner) Atsushi Onita being carved open by barbed wire and blown up by small explosive devices. Indeed, no FMW bill was complete without a headlining bout that featured enough bloodshed to put a particularly gnarly episode of *Casualty* to shame.

For one event, Onita embellished FMW's trademark gimmicks by promoting a show in which the ring was placed on a floating platform in the middle of an Olympic-size swimming pool. The main event was, incredibly, billed as a 'no-rope electrified explosive barbed wire double hell swimming pool deathmatch'. Members of each team were eliminated when they were thrown from the ring into the water, at which point huge explosions would be set off adjacent to where they landed. It looked spectacular although had no ill-effect on the grapplers, given that they were submerged when the bombs were detonated – which rendered the bout's central conceit entirely pointless.

After a blood-soaked brawl that also involved a baseball bat wrapped in barbed wire, a kama (a type of Japanese sickle) and, courtesy of Mr Pogo, a pair of fireballs, Onita flung Hideki Hosaka into the electrified barbed wire and then powerbombed him for the winning pinfall. The victorious fighter motored back to poolside in an inflatable dinghy, after which he received the medical attention that was necessitated by almost every one of his matches: during his career, he required a cumulative total of over 1,000 stitches.

Jerry Lawler vs Terry Funk

SURREAL

Memphis, Tennessee, April 1981

Ferocious rivals contest a fight to the finish in completely empty 11,000-seat arena

'I can't see! Doctor! God help me, please help me!' wailed Terry Funk, clutching his eye as blood streamed down his face. So ended his April 1981 match with Jerry 'The King' Lawler, which took place in an entirely desolate 11,000-seat Mid-South Coliseum. Funk had complained that the fans and referees in Memphis were so biased towards local hero Lawler that the only way the two could have a fair fight was if it was witnessed only by a cameraman, photographer and announcer to document what happened. This was the premise for their Continental Wrestling Association 'empty arena' contest, which was filmed on a Monday afternoon prior to the promotion's regular weekly show in the venue.

The performance began before either wrestler arrived, with commentator Lance Russell doing a completely straight piece-to-camera in which he made out that he didn't even know if the contestants would show up. A few minutes later, Funk lurched towards the ring, from where he hurled an avalanche of ad-libbed abuse at Russell, who chastised him for swearing. 'I don't give a shit!' responded Funk. When Lawler finally emerged from the opposite end of the deserted arena, he appeared to have forgotten that no fans were in attendance and was clad in his usual wrestling attire of tights, cape and crown. Funk later said that it was the most absurd thing he'd ever seen.

Once the two adversaries were in the ring, they circled each other slowly, with Funk expertly projecting the impression that he was completely out of control and had every intention of injuring Lawler. They began the violent ballet by flailing wildly, before rolling out of the ring and throwing each other into the unoccupied seats at ringside. Funk then pummelled Lawler with a metal section marker, piledrove him on the floor and – while dementedly shrieking 'kill him!' – slammed his face into a table.

BLOOD

The apparently maniacal Funk then destroyed the wooden ring steps, retrieved a large spike from the debris and yelled, 'I'm gonna get his eye!' as he attempted to stab 'The King' in the face. Russell abandoned his commentary position in a bid to reason with Funk. But Lawler escaped his opponent's grasp and kicked Funk, who was still clutching the spike, in the stomach. The blow caused Funk to recoil and, so viewers were led to believe, inadvertently jab himself in the eye with the pointy stick. Funk fell to the mat, holding his hands to his face as he screamed like a wounded (albeit spandex-clad) animal. And that was how the match ended. With no referee, no victor was declared although it's generally considered that Lawler 'officially' won the melee due to Funk's inability to continue.

Lawler exited the ring, collected his cape and crown, and walked out of the arena, which prompted his 'blinded' adversary to wail, 'Lawler, come back here, you yellow pig!' So persuasive was Funk's act that television viewers were convinced he had suffered a genuine eye injury. Funk later derided the entire concept as a 'dumb idea' as it resulted in zero box office takings. Nonetheless, it inspired the empty arena contest between Mick 'Mankind' Foley and Dwayne 'The Rock' Johnson that was broadcast during the half-time interval of Super Bowl XXXIII in January 1999 and was, at the time, the most-watched WWF match ever on US cable television.

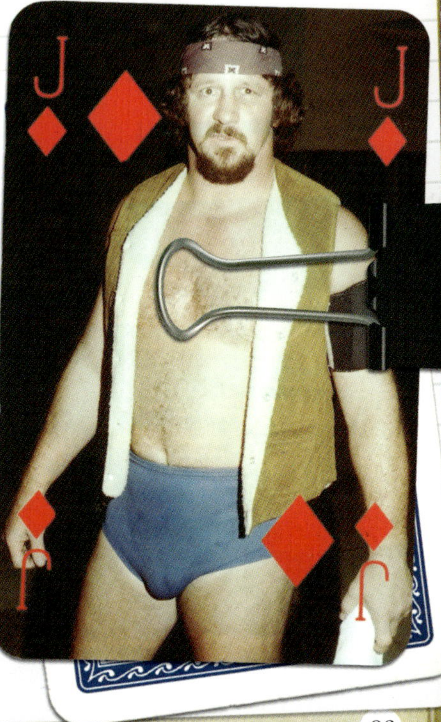

Tarzan Goto & Mr Gannosuke vs Shoji Nakamaki & Keisuke Yamada

Tokyo, Japan, August 1995

WATER

Tag match in Japanese bath house culminates with deadly shampoo assault

Japanese promotion IWA may have, like FMW, been best known for its gory matches based around barbed wire and explosives. But its oddest moment came when it ran a pair of tag team matches in a public bath house. A wrestling mat was set up in the lobby area and, in order to win, you had to pin a member of the opposing team and then dunk his head under water for five seconds. The team members that weren't tagged in had to sit in a Jacuzzi in an adjoining room, while still wearing their wrestling gear.

In the opening bout, Tarzan Goto and Mr Gannosuke defeated The Headhunters (a pair of identical twins with a combined weight of around 650lbs) by disqualification when one of the 'Hunters crawled out of the hot tub as he was unable to cope with the heat. This was swiftly followed by a contest in which Goto and Gannosuke faced Keisuke Yamada and Shoji Nakamaki.

The heavyweights brawled all over the bath house, which sent myriads of naked women fleeing in terror. Goto flung wicker baskets at Yamada, which he sold as if he'd been hit with a sledgehammer, before thwacking Nakamaki with a broom. As the bout progressed, a bath house attendant placed more wood in the furnace heating the hot tubs: Nakamaki and Gannosuke gave the impression that they were being boiled alive, while waiting to be tagged back into the match.

Goto won the bout for his team after he poured shampoo on Yamada and lathered his head and upper body. The Headhunters then ran back into the building and instigated a six-way brawl, during which Goto rubbed Yamada's face into the naked breasts of a number of unfortunate female bathers. The fracas ended with all six wrestlers fighting in the street in front of bemused passers-by.

Crash Holly vs The Headbangers

Long Island, New York, March 2000

'Houdini of Hardcore' retains championship by fleeing into amusement park ball pool

SURREAL

Comedy

The WWF was not often associated with the concept of surreal whimsy although that was precisely what it offered during the multiple hardcore title reigns of Crash Holly during 2000-2002. The championship was, in fact, a battered old WWF title belt from the late 1980s that was held together with duct tape and had the words 'Hardcore Champion' scrawled on it in marker pen.

During Holly's numerous stints as champion, a 24/7 rule was implemented, which meant that, as long as a referee was on hand, Holly could be challenged for the title whatever the time or place. Cue a series of skits in which the unsuspecting 'Houdini of Hardcore' was attacked in locations ranging from a hotel room in the dead of night to a luggage carousel at Newark Airport.

The highlight of the series was a scrap involving the tag team of Mosh and Thrasher, collectively known as The Headbangers, at Long Island amusement park Fun Time USA. It began with Mosh heading to the upstairs area of the entertainment complex, where he found Crash playing an arcade game. Cameraman in tow, Crash escaped down a slide, only to walk straight into Thrasher, who bashed him across the face with a metal dustbin.

The Headbangers followed up by using poor Crash's head in lieu of a mallet on a test your strength machine, before Crash fled into a ball pool. The pursuing tag partners agreed that they would 'get him in the balls'. But Holly pre-empted them with a flying clothesline and a rope swing-assisted huracanrana, after which he raced out of the front door to retain the championship.

Antonio Inoki vs Masa Saito

EPIC

Ganryujima Island, Japan, October 1987

Samurai duel inspires Japanese wrestlers to have two-hour match on deserted island

New Japan Pro Wrestling's Antonio Inoki wanted to do something unusual to mark the start of the new Japanese television season in October 1987. For inspiration, he looked to the samurai Musashi Miyamoto and Kojiro Sasaki, who fought a duel to the death in 1612 on a tiny uninhabited island in Japan's Kanmon Straits.

He decided to promote a match in the same location between himself and nemesis Masa Saito, with no referee, no rules and no fans in attendance (only television cameramen and photographers saw the match live). It was dubbed, somewhat ostentatiously, a 'jungle island deathmatch'.

BLOOD

Inoki also had the notion that, for the bout to be really memorable, it needed to be incredibly long. As such, much of the contest consisted of the two wrestlers circling each other in slow motion without actually doing anything. When they did lock up, they would exchange headlocks while rolling around in the grass surrounding the ring, as if they were taking part in a particularly well-funded school fight. As the light faded, huge flaming torches were lit. Inoki attempted to throw his opponent into one of them, knocking it to the ground, while Saito later retaliated by clonking Inoki with a length of wood.

With both contestants bleeding liberally, proceedings finally came to an end when Inoki caught Saito in a choke hold. He was declared the winner by technical knockout after a staggering two hours and five minutes. An exhausted Inoki collapsed to the ground, while Saito was stretchered off. At no point during the bout was there any indication that they were anywhere near a jungle.

CM Punk vs Chavo Guerrero

Corpus Christi, Texas, February 2008

Street fight ends when WWE star is hurled into the Gulf of Mexico

One of WWE's most peculiar stipulation matches took place in Corpus Christi, Texas when CM Punk faced Chavo Guerrero in what was billed as a Gulf of Mexico bout. Pins or submissions meant nothing here: the only way to defeat your opponent was to throw him into the bay adjacent to the arena.

The contest started off in a traditional manner, with both participants in the ring. But they soon headed out of the squared circle, over the barrier at ringside and into the crowd. Guerrero dominated the brawl and launched Punk into a row of seats, before they disappeared from view into the venue's foyer.

The camera crew finally caught up with the combatants in the backstage area, which they fought through before heading out of a side door and into the car park. A pre-arranged flourish saw a car skid to a halt as they battled in front of it, allowing Guerrero to fling Punk on to the bonnet. The two grapplers continued to fight their way towards the waterfront, where Punk backdropped Guerrero into the windscreen of a parked van.

A few (presumably highly bemused) fishermen looked on as Guerrero lobbed their cool box at Punk's head, after which he attempted to suplex the 'straight edge superstar' into the marina. Punk escaped the hold and struck back by kneeing Guerrero in the face with his GTS finisher – the force of which sent Guerrero soaring into the water. The defeated wrestler splashed about desperately in a bid to suggest that he was drowning, before he was pulled out of the bay by scuba divers.

BLOOD
MUTILATION
Shopping list
Beer
Vodka
More beer
Nurofen
IMPROMPTU FINISH
DOOMED CONCEPT

CHAPTER 5:

FREAKS AND GEEKS

Sandman, Raven, Tommy Dreamer & Yoshihiro Tajiri vs Rhino, Steve Corino, Jack Victory & Scotty Anton

Pensacola, Florida, June 2000

Intoxicated mat maniac brings main event to a halt by dropping trousers

DRUNKENNESS

Jim 'Sandman' Fullington was primarily known for two things during his wrestling career: hitting opponents extremely hard with the kendo stick he carried to the ring and drinking – a lot. During his stints in the original incarnation of the Philadelphia-based Extreme Championship Wrestling, he would stay up all weekend and combine the Friday and Saturday night shows with monumental booze sessions. It wasn't unusual for him to arrive in a dressing room equipped with 48 cans of beer. Even his signature moves – the White Russian legsweep and the Heinekenrana – were named after his preferred beverages.

Prior to an eight-man main event at an untelevised show in June 2000, though, Fullington managed to get *really* plastered by virtue of having downed almost two litres of vodka. He entered the auditorium through the crowd, while smoking and pouring beer into fans' mouths – all of which was a traditional part of his act. As he jumped over the ringside barrier, he unintentionally fell to the floor. It was only a hint of the debacle to come.

After stumbling down the aisle, he finally made it into the ring, at which point he grabbed the microphone and yelled, 'Fuck these guys, let's go and check out a bar!' The four members of the opposing team stood outside the ring, waiting for Fullington to calm down. In a bid to buy some time, Tommy Dreamer bellowed over the PA, 'It's plain and simple, why don't you four pussies get in the ring and we'll kick your fuckin' ass? And when we're done kicking your ass, we're all going to go to the bar and watch Sandman get naked!'

Unfortunately, this planted an idea in Fullington's grog-addled mind and he then stood in the centre of the ring and pulled down his jeans and underwear. Just as he was about to lift his T-shirt up to give the audience a clearer view of his tackle, Dreamer intervened and pulled his briefs up. With Sandman's clothing back in place, Dreamer and Raven grabbed either end of the rope that Raven had brought to the ring and swung it round while Sandman skipped over it.

A semblance of a match subsequently started when Sandman's team ran up the aisle to tussle with the rival squad. Sandman then charged back into the ring and slipped over, before throwing a table into the squared circle and lying down on it. A visibly annoyed Steve Corino said into the mic, 'I'm a nice guy. Let him pass out, we'll work around him, let's have a traditional match.' Fullington responded by again dropping his trousers and mooning Rhino. He then cracked an unsuspecting Victory over the head with his cane at full pelt.

The dipsomaniac finally lurched backstage and the remaining grapplers were able to start the match properly. This lasted for about a minute before Fullington returned clutching a case of Budweiser. He then wandered around the venue downing lager and smashing the empty cans over his own head as the other wrestlers continued with the match, which Sandman's team won when Dreamer pinned Rhino. Backstage after the shambolic main event, Victory expressed his anger at Fullington for hitting him so hard with the kendo stick, which led to a scuffle in the toilets. Sandman jabbed his fingers in Victory's eyes, who retaliated with a series of headbutts. Unsurprisingly, Fullington awoke the following day with no recollection of the previous night's japes.

Shopping list
Beer
Vodka
More beer
Nurofen

JR Benson vs John Pierce

San Francisco, California, October 1995

Valet revives 'knocked out' wrestler by urinating on him in middle of street

URINE

Wrestling often makes promises it's unable to deliver on, whether it's a loser-must-retire stipulation that is never adhered to or a sub-standard 'mystery opponent'. But cult outfit Incredibly Strange Wrestling – created by rockabilly musician and film producer Johnny Legend, although quickly taken over by local promoter Audra Angeli-Morse – resolutely lived up to its name. A fixture of San Francisco's club scene from 1995–2001, it offered a chaotic DIY punk aesthetic and an outrageous array of vaguely lucha libre-inspired characters, such as El Homo Loco ('The Crazy Homo'), the Ku Klux Klown and El Pollo Diablo ('The Devil Chicken'). All of which helped to secure the lo-fi outfit slots on touring music festivals such as Lollapalooza and the Vans Warped Tour.

Unlike the majority of grapplers on the roster, the most deranged character in the promotion's early days didn't rely on an absurd pseudonym or a costume purchased from the nearest fancy dress shop. Local indie wrestler JR Benson was more concerned with what madcap stunts he could perform in ISW that would be unthinkable elsewhere – not whether he was wearing a chicken costume while doing it. A June 1995 main event between Benson and John Pierce culminated with Pierce 'knocking out' his adversary with a folding chair. Benson's valet revived her charge by removing her panties and rubbing them in his face.

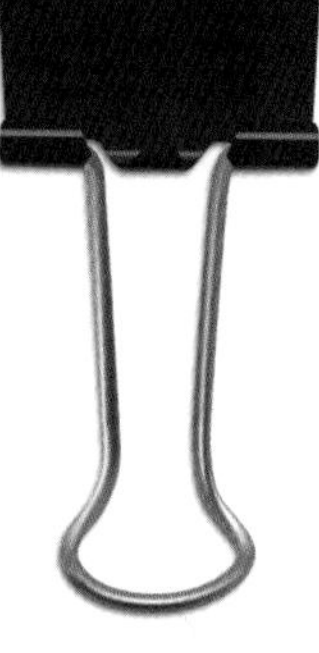

A falls-count-anywhere rematch between Benson and Pierce – held in a club named the Transmission Theatre in San Francisco's SoMa district – took place four months later. It began with a brief series of first-day-at-wrestling-school exchanges, after which Pierce clocked JR with a stiff chair shot. He then sat Benson on the chair and, in the first vaguely professional looking move, hit him with a flying cross-body block. Pierce continued to dominate the match with more chair-based offence, as the referee – incongruously clad in a wrestling mask and black karate gi – looked on nonchalantly. When the bartender called for last orders over the PA, it only added to the surreal cadence of proceedings.

Benson retaliated with a kick to Pierce's stomach, which he followed up with a tope (a dive through the ropes). Back in the ring, Benson rolled up his rival for the winning three-count – somewhat undermining the whole falls-count-anywhere stipulation. If the match itself was anticlimactic, the follow-up was anything but. Pierce's second, Mistress Stacey, clobbered Benson's own valet, Jenny X, with a chair, which she sold as if she had been knocked unconscious. With barely a moment's hesitation, Benson revived his manager by – with the aid of a torch – simulating cunnilingus on her.

Still smarting from his loss, Pierce then resumed combat with Benson, taking their pseudo-fight through the audience and out of the club's front door on to 11th Street. As baffled passers-by looked on, they brawled down the pavement, throwing worked punches at one another. Stacey then pummelled Benson with yet another chair shot, causing him to crumple to the ground beside a busy intersection. In order to 'resuscitate' JR, Jenny X squatted over him and urinated on his face. The bizarre spectacle ended with Benson and X running off down the street, presumably to avoid arrest. All four participants were later fired for their involvement in the stunt and Benson went on to form a rival promotion, which he dubbed Extremely Strange Wrestling.

King Kong Bundy, Lord Littlebrook & Little Tokyo vs Hillbilly Jim, Haiti Kid & Little Beaver

Pontiac, Michigan, March 1987

Huge bad guy attacks midget to the surreal soundtrack of utterly misguided commentary

WrestleMania III remains the most iconic American wrestling show ever, thanks to the stunning visual of a stadium packed with 78,000 fans and the superbly hyped main event of Hulk Hogan vs Andre the Giant.

What's less well remembered is its patchy undercard and the bizarre spectacle that pitted the team of King Kong Bundy, Lord Littlebrook and Little Tokyo against Hillbilly Jim, Haiti Kid and Little Beaver. The huge, bald-headed Bundy looked like an evil George Dawes, while the equally massive Hillbilly Jim affected the appearance of a happy-go-lucky bumpkin, replete with dungarees and unkempt beard. The other four participants were midgets. The entire confrontation was centred on the comedy visual of placing some really big blokes in the ring with some really little ones.

The match began with basic exchanges between the four vertically-challenged grapplers, before Bundy and Hillbilly clobbered one another in what looked like slow motion. As the bald-headed bad guy began to dominate proceedings, the cluster of amateur-looking sequences was brought to a suitably cheap conclusion when Little Beaver interfered on his partner's behalf. Bundy – who was solely meant to face off against Hillbilly – retaliated by dropping an elbow on his small-scale opponent, only to be promptly disqualified by the referee for perpetrating such a heinous act.

Comedy

The whole sorry episode was given a further peculiar twist thanks to the wondrously-misguided guest commentary from former baseball star Bob Uecker, who made no effort to disguise the fact that he knew nothing about pro wrestling. At one point he even yelped, 'Hey, Little Beaver just gave Bundy a shot in the boiler,' surely one of the more improbable phrases you're ever likely to hear.

Stalker Ichikawa vs Amazing Kong

Tokyo, Japan, May 2005

Disturbingly-attired groper summarily flattened by gargantuan female opposition

Perennial loser Stalker Ichikawa rocks quite the look. On top of a black Lycra bodysuit, he dons a PVC cape, which is complemented by an open-face balaclava on to which have been Velcroed a pair of foot-long ears. The final flourish is a plastic trident that he carries on his approach to the ring (which is soundtracked by the 'William Tell Overture' - possibly the least likely wrestling entrance theme ever). The overall aesthetic is that of a child's Halloween costume gone terribly wrong.

For his bout against ferocious female wrestler Amazing Kong, he also wore a soft toy in the shape of a donkey around his waist, which he affected to 'ride' down the aisle. Suffice to say, as he entered the ring, Kong's response - in between doing her best not to laugh - was one of dumbfounded incredulity.

Once the bell rang, Ichikawa (billed weight: 84lbs) attacked Kong (billed weight: 231lbs) with a flurry of karate chops, to no effect whatsoever. Frustrated - perhaps in more ways than one - Ichikawa then decided to squeeze his opponent's breasts. Kong's look of boredom swiftly changed to one of outrage, at which point she clobbered the aptly-named Stalker in the throat and then clotheslined him to the mat. The pinfall was a mere formality and the entire bout lasted just 20 seconds.

Unwilling to concede defeat, Ichikawa immediately challenged Kong to a two-on-one rematch, this time with the equally deluded DJ Nira as his partner. Their efforts were met with little success - Nira fled the ring at one point - although Stalker did manage to hit Kong with his trademark manoeuvre of poking his opponent in the arse with his index fingers. The fearsome lady-wrestler retaliated with a match-winning splash off the top rope, after which she marched straight back to the dressing room - presumably vowing never to wrestle a man strapped to a toy donkey ever again.

Lance Steel vs Darkness Crabtree

Reading/Emmaus, Pennsylvania, October 2004

No time-limit match purportedly lasts for almost 24 hours

Chikara isn't like other American wrestling promotions. Whereas WWE is largely based around hulking behemoths who appear to take what they do very seriously indeed, Chikara - a small indie league based in Philadelphia - features average-sized blokes with names such as Dasher Hatfield or El Hijo del Ice Cream mucking about in ridiculous-looking Mexican wrestling-style masks.

Matches from Chikara (which is Japanese for strength) offer a compelling mix of cataclysmic gymnastics and slapstick comedy: this is the promotion in which a bout was once interrupted due to a 'local ninja school' invading the arena. One of the outfit's wackiest creations was the character of Darkness Crabtree, a decrepit old man clad in a blue mask with furry white trim, designed to mimic the remaining wisps of hair you would expect of an octogenarian - his debut match was billed as having taken place in 1937 and his not-exactly-snappy nickname was the 'Cranky Curmudgeon of the Squared Circle'.

Given that he struggled even to enter the ring for his match against Lance Steel, it seemed unlikely that he had much chance of victory. Indeed, Steel pinned him in just 13 seconds. Aggrieved, Crabtree asked for the microphone and complained, 'I've not even woke up yet. How about the best two out of three?' It took Steel 10 seconds to win a second fall. Crabtree, smarting from the loss, then suggested an immediate rematch, this time under submission rules. Steel was happy to oblige and placed Darkness in a side headlock, causing him to tap out in eight seconds.

Comedy

'Let's have a hardcore match,' said Crabtree. 'You wait in the middle and I'll get a table.' As Darkness began to exit the ring to fetch said piece of furniture, Steel pinned him with a backslide, this time in just six seconds. Crabtree demanded a falls-count-anywhere match, which took Steel an epic 27 seconds to win.

The by-now perennial loser then had one final request: a contest with no count-outs and no time limit. Incredibly, Steel didn't win in a matter of seconds. Instead, the two masked grapplers fought their way out of the ring and through the fire exit into the car park, referee in tow. They disappeared round the side of the building and weren't seen for the rest of the night. The show eventually ended without the match having any conclusion.

Chikara ran another show 35 miles away the following evening. Just after the event's first match had ended, Steel, Crabtree and referee crashed into the hall through a side door as a bemused audience looked on. Crabtree threw Steel into the ring, only to be hit by a chop that sent him plummeting to the mat. Steel then placed his felled opponent in a Boston crab, which forced Darkness to submit. The official time of the match: 23 hours and 36 minutes.

Necro Butcher vs Lufisto

Toronto, Canada, October 2006

Female wrestler wins deathmatch tournament by attacking hillbilly with fluorescent light tubes

Away from the ring, Dylan Summers is a softly-spoken and thoughtful father of two. Inside the ring, he's a barefoot, hillbilly maniac known as the Necro Butcher who specialises in ultraviolent deathmatches. As anyone who saw his cameo appearance in Oscar-nominated drama *The Wrestler* will attest, his modus operandi is not for the squeamish. A typical Necro Butcher bout tends to involve a baroque arsenal of weaponry that includes staple guns, fluorescent light tubes and huge spider webs of barbed wire. He once set fire to his own trousers before executing a legdrop on his equally hapless opponent. But his most ludicrously distasteful moment was a 2006 match in which he faced female wrestler Lufisto in the final of Canada's first ever deathmatch tournament, an event dubbed *Bloodstock*.

Butcher began proceedings by clobbering Lufisto across the head with the championship belt she carried to the ring. He then flung her into a wall. Lufisto retaliated by throwing Necro down a flight of concrete steps. After that entrée of violence, the deathmatch rivals clambered into the ring, which was filled with so many boxes of fluorescent tubes - the weapon of choice in underground hardcore bouts - that it could have been confused for B&Q's lighting aisle.

With Necro slumped in the corner following a series of punches, Lufisto positioned a cluster of taped-together light tubes in front of his head and kneed him in the face, shattering the glass cylinders in the process – a truly revolting sight. The 5ft 3in, 140lb Lufisto continued the assault by smashing further tubes over Necro's head, stomach and back, causing him to bleed profusely from dozens of tiny cuts. She then wiped Summers' blood over her own body, before shoving him into the barbed wire that was wrapped around the ropes.

Despite the abundance of abuse that Necro had taken, he managed a suitably vicious riposte by slamming Lufisto across the top of two steel chairs placed back-to-back. This was followed by a set piece in which the two seemingly deranged grapplers sat facing one other and took it in turns to punch each other, hard, in the face. Necro then balanced over a dozen fluorescent tubes between the two chairs and attempted to powerbomb Lufisto through them. Fortunately for her, the script called for Lufisto (real name Genevieve Goulet) to escape from the hold and execute a suplex of her own into the tubes, followed by the pinfall and tournament victory. By the time the bout was concluded, both wrestlers were swathed in blood and shards of broken glass.

Lufisto, the lone woman in the tournament, was only able to participate in it after the Ontario Human Rights Commission petitioned to overturn a ruling that banned women from wrestling men in the province: a regulation by the local athletic commission (part of Canada's Ministry of Consumer Affairs) had stated, 'No person shall hold a professional contest or exhibition of wrestling where male and female wrestlers are in the ring at the same time.' Whether the Ontario Human Rights Commission grasped that it had won Goulet the right to fight blokes in ultraviolent deathmatches remains to be seen.

Ryuma Go vs Uchu Majin Silver X

Tokyo, Japan, April 1995

Cult hero fends off hockey mask-clad alien before crowd of 50,000

When Japanese magazine *Weekly Pro Wrestling* ran an ambitious multi-promotion show at the Tokyo Dome in April 1995, it wasn't just mainstream leagues such as New Japan and All Japan Pro Wrestling that were handed the opportunity to show their wares in front of a sold-out crowd of 50,000 fans. Further down the card, in a bout from cult promotion Go Gundan, Ryuma Go faced an 'alien' (actually a bloke in a poorly-fitting hockey mask) called Uchu Majin Silver X, who was accompanied by a pair of *Doctor Who*-style baddies clad in dungarees.

It was one of the most amateurish-looking bouts to have ever taken place on a major wrestling show. While the first goon distracted the referee, his partner freely interfered on X's behalf. On the rare occasions that Go, who won after 15 minutes of this nonsense, did manage to squeeze in any offence, it generally consisted of clotheslines and headbutting the bloke who was wearing a hockey mask – something that, even by the standards of pro wrestling, demonstrated an astounding lack of logic.

Despite his uncanny knack for fending off extraterrestrials, Go (a former WWF junior heavyweight champion) later fell on hard times. Before his death in October 2009, he appeared in a number of Japanese porn flicks and was arrested in January 2003 for stealing a 69-year-old woman's handbag at Shinjuku train station. Perhaps having aliens clobber you with steel chairs wasn't such a bad way to make a living after all.

Martín Karadagián vs La Momia

Buenos Aires, Argentina, October 1972

Argentina's most popular wrestler ever meets his match in *Scooby-Doo*-style baddie

Martín Karadagián was a squat, middle-aged man who looked unremarkable save for his prominent nose and the comical contrast of his dyed blond hair and black beard. He was also Argentina's most popular wrestler ever, a mainstream celebrity whose weekly appearances on the show *Titanes en el Ring* generated the country's highest television ratings in the early 1970s.

While American groups of the era still tried to portray wrestling as a sport, *Titanes en el Ring* had no such ambitions: there were no attempts at realism and its heavily-choreographed main events pitted Karadagián against an iniquitous cast of *Scooby-Doo*-style monsters.

Karadagián found his greatest success in a feud with La Momia ('The Mummy'). The character was portrayed by opening match wrestler Gitano Ivanoff who, predictably enough, was enveloped from head to toe in bandages. La Momia never felt any pain (presumably a handy side-effect of being dead), never spoke and always won by placing a supposedly devastating nerve hold on opponents.

His 1972 showdown with Karadagián marked the peak of wrestling's popularity in Argentina – it attracted a crowd of 22,000 – and was one of the worst matches ever. Karadagián began the fight by charging at his foe and clobbering him with weak-looking blows. La Momia retaliated by attempting to strangle Karadagián, who then began to attack Momia's lower back – the first time an offensive manoeuvre ever had any discernable effect on the reanimated corpse.

The rest of the bout consisted of the two wrestlers throwing delicate punches at one another, in between the mummy staggering around the ring in a ludicrous fashion and intermittently wrapping his hands around Karadagián's throat. The whole performance, which was so surreal that Karadagián was struggling not to laugh, ended in a no-contest when the rest of the roster ran into the ring and pulled Karadagián and his undead nemesis apart. Inexplicably, the two rivals then hugged one another, proving that it's just not possible to stay mad for long at a man who is so comprehensively swathed in bandages.

Big Show vs Akebono

Fans turn on stage-managed sumo match at **WrestleMania** before it even starts

Los Angeles, California, April 2005

DOOMED CONCEPT

WrestleMania is WWE's biggest event of the year, a show on which storylines culminate in the most enticing matches that the promotion can muster. But in filling out the card, the organisation doesn't always get it right. To wit, this hilariously misjudged 'sumo' match at **WrestleMania 21**, in which the almost 7ft-tall WWE star the Big Show faced retired sumo wrestler Akebono, the first ever non-Japanese fighter to reach the sport's highest rank of **yokozuna** (grand champion).

The 6ft 8in, 500lb Akebono (born Chadwick Rowan in Waimanalo, Hawaii) became a huge celebrity in Japan thanks to his sumo success throughout the 1990s but was a virtual unknown in the US. His only previous WWE match was a brief warm-up contest a week earlier. The trappings of his fixed fight against the Big Show were designed to replicate those of a genuine sumo contest as closely as possible... but the live audience couldn't have been less interested. The ring ropes were removed and, in a hilariously low-rent attempt to replicate a **dohyo** (sumo ring), a gym mat – on to which a large black

ABSURD COSTUME

circle had been daubed - was placed over the canvas. To win, you had to push your opponent outside the circle or knock him off his feet.

The Big Show came to the ring dressed in possibly the largest kimono ever created. It soon became apparent that he wasn't taking the performance seriously - he rolled up the bottom of his robe to flash some leg on his way down the aisle and, once in the ring, he winked at ringside fans. The wrestlers removed their kimonos to reveal that they were both clad only in **mawashis**, traditional sumo belts, as fans in the arena jeered. The attempts at authenticity also extended to a protracted ceremony before the fight that included salt throwing, hand clapping, foot stomping and gut patting, as referee Ren Urano (who later reprised his role as a sumo ref in **Ocean's Thirteen**) sang into a folding fan. Indeed, the pre-match rituals lasted far longer than the match itself would and, with no sign of the faffing coming to an end, the audience started booing and yelling 'boring!' - a rare instance of fans bellowing such a chant **before** a contest has even started.

The two fatties finally crouched down opposite each other and charged forwards to mark the start of the tussle. After shoving each other furiously in the chest, they bumped bellies, as if doing their best Big Daddy impressions. They collided again and, jockeying for position, each grappler seized his opponent's **mawashi** as the ref bawled at them in Japanese. After finding little success with a shoulder tackle, the Big Show then roared and raised his right hand, as if he was about to chokeslam his colossal adversary.

Instead, he lifted Akebono off the ground briefly and placed him near the edge of the ring. But the former sumo champion used his opponent's supposed momentum to hurl him out of ring and to the floor. As the vanquished giant tumbled to the ground, TV viewers were met with the appalling sight of an almost full-screen shot of his enormous arse. The entire contest was over in just one minute and two seconds. Akebono went on to work for bonkers Japanese pro wrestling group Hustle, where he played the role of Monster Bono - a giant, dummy-sucking baby that was conceived when face-painted wrestler the Great Muta blew green mist into the crotch of a model billed as Yinling the Erotic Terrorist.

Thumbtack Jack vs DJ Hyde

Townsend, Delaware, June 2009

Wrestler wins deathmatch tournament despite being stabbed in face with syringe

The first time you watch a fluorescent light tube being smashed over someone's head is an unsettling experience. But for wrestlers involved in Combat Zone Wrestling's horrifically violent *Tournament of Death*, light tubes are the least of their worries. The underground event pits around a dozen hardcore grapplers against one another in matches that are as creative as they are graphic, with barbed wire, staple guns and cheese graters all frequently used as weapons. While the results may be pre-arranged, the sadistic routines within each bout can be horribly real.

Thumbtack Jack's first round match again DJ Hyde in the 2009 tournament began predictably enough: Hyde fell face-first into broken glass; Jack was flung through half-a-dozen light tubes. Then things got really sick.

Hyde carved open Jack's forehead with a butterfly knife and - in the pièce de résistance - shoved a syringe into his mouth. Hyde forced the needle through his opponent's left cheek, before he hit the plunger and shot the syringe's contents across the ring. With the first syringe still hanging from Jack's face, Hyde repeated the stunt with the other cheek. He then compounded Jack's agony by powerbombing him through a pane of glass that was on fire.

Jack gained a measure of revenge when he jammed six acupuncture needles into the top of DJ's head and hit him in the face with a cinder block, after which he finally brought the carnage to an end with the winning three-count. The 23-year-old went on to win the tournament when the other finalist, Nick Gage, had to be airlifted to hospital after he severed an artery just below his armpit.

Jake Roberts vs JT Lightning

Lakewood, Ohio, September 2008

Inebriated 1980s star follows unscheduled loss by punching wall and breaking hand

It didn't bode well. Just before he was due to appear in the main event of a show promoted by Firestorm Pro Wrestling, former WWF star Jake 'The Snake' Roberts was found passed out backstage, with two empty vodka bottles by his bag. When he was woken up, he angrily demanded an 8-ball of cocaine.

Despite being out of his mind on booze, Roberts still made it to the ring for his match with local wrestler JT Lightning – although he needn't have bothered. After delivering a garbled monologue over the PA, he struggled even to make it through the ropes. Lightning's instinct was to attempt to guide Roberts through a basic contest but within seconds it became apparent that 'The Snake' was incapable even of that, after he resolutely failed to sell the forearm blows that Lightning was throwing at him. Roberts then backed into a corner and JT attempted to place him in a headlock, only for Roberts to drop face-first to the mat.

With no hope of salvaging the contest, Lightning forced Roberts' shoulders to the canvas and – contrary to the pre-planned conclusion – told the referee to count to three, ending the match in just over two minutes. A livid JT then grabbed the mic and declared that Roberts was 'a piece of shit', after which the intoxicated 53-year-old returned to the dressing room area, punched a wall and broke his hand, before he ran into the street crying. Roberts' assistant later released a statement suggesting that someone at the event had spiked the veteran grappler's drink.

IMPROMPTU FINISH

Magic Man vs Jinsei Shinzaki

Sendai, Japan, January 1998

Comedy

Hapless novelty act vows to end losing streak, only to be defeated in five seconds

It was never 'Magic Man' Jack Sinn's idea to become a wrestler. As a manager on the mid-1990s US independent scene, his modus operandi was to interfere on his charge's behalf by distracting the referee with an arsenal of magic tricks. He'd occasionally have to perform a few pratfalls but he had no first-hand experience of executing a match – something he made clear to Japanese promotion Michinoku Pro Wrestling when they booked him to appear on a series of shows in the summer of 1997.

Sinn arrived in Japan anticipating that his role as an extra would entail nothing more dangerous than some sleight of hand. But the troupe was one grappler short after Vampiro – a huge star in Mexico – pulled out of the tour, citing an injury. And with that, Magic Man went from ringside distraction to fully-fledged grappler. 'I was scared to death because these guys really knew what they were doing, they did a lot of high-flying,' says Sinn. 'And I was thinking, "Oh no, I'm going to get killed." And sure enough, in the first couple of matches, they really beat the heck out of me. I'd never been properly trained: it was trial by fire.'

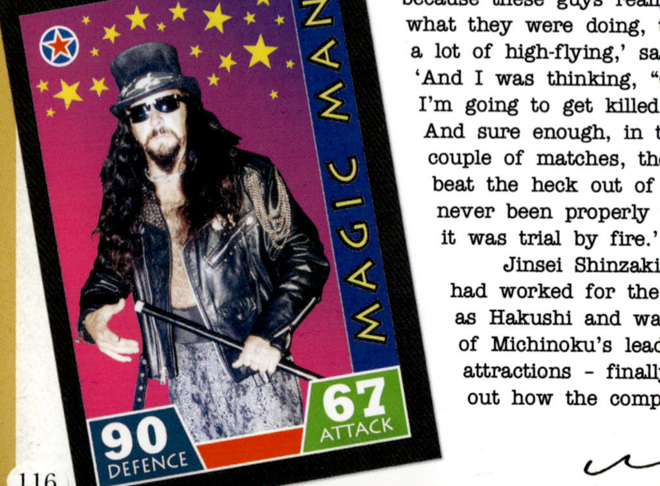

Jinsei Shinzaki – who had worked for the WWF as Hakushi and was one of Michinoku's leading attractions – finally figured out how the company could best utilise the American conjuror. 'I didn't know how to wrestle so they had me come out to the ring and do a magic show,' says Sinn. 'Then when the match started, I would try to do my cheating stuff. I had a cane that disappeared, I was constantly trying to throw salt in people's eyes – which was just a little bag of baby powder – or shoot fireballs at them. And then I'd get my ass kicked.'

The act was effective enough that, by the end of the year, Magic Man was placed in a feud with Shinzaki – although he found little success. Before one bout, he 'hypnotised' his opponent and then performed a song-and-dance routine. 'Shinzaki could really keep a straight face even while I was doing the silliest stuff,' says Sinn. 'As soon as I woke him up, he chopped me in the throat and I went over the top rope out into the fans. I was coughing and gasping for air, while the fans, in between laughing, were trying to hold me up.' Another contest ended when a towel was thrown in, to prevent Magic Man from taking a further beating.

The series between the two was due to culminate with a bout on 14 January 1998, which was billed as Magic Man's 'revenge' match. There would be no stoppages and pinfalls counted anywhere. But when Sinn arrived at the venue, Shinzaki informed him, 'Magic Man, tonight we take it easy.' The Japanese grappler had suffered a back injury while working for another promotion and was in no condition to perform. 'So he decided that I would do a really long magic show,' says Sinn. 'And then before the match, I got the ring announcer to say that I'd been training really hard and I knew I could finally beat Shinzaki tonight. I was shaking the ropes and going nuts, while the crowd was getting more and more hyped up. And then they rang they bell.'

As planned, Magic Man and Shinzaki ran towards one another and collided in the centre of the ring. Sinn fell straight to the mat and Shinzaki lay on top of him to secure the winning three-count in a record-setting 5.49 seconds. 'It was all Shinzaki could do because his back was hurting him really bad,' says Sinn. 'After the match, I rolled out of the ring and threw a fit, I cried, kicked my feet and acted like a big sissy. But I got paid my regular pay just to take one bump.'

GENUINE
POW
FIGHT
DR DEATH
INJURY
IMPROMPTU FINISH

CHAPTER 6:

THROWING THE SCRIPT OUT

Kurt Angle vs Daniel Puder

St Louis, Missouri, November 2004

WWE reality series goes awry when contestant almost defeats top star in real fight

Tough Enough never really worked. In the WWE reality TV show, participants would be trained as wrestlers and compete for a contract with the organisation, with the idea that a new star would be instantly created. But it takes months, if not years, to be ready to appear in WWE rings and no one came out of the series as an overnight star. By the fourth and final season in late 2004, *Tough Enough* had been dropped as a standalone programme by MTV and the weekly episodes were instead incorporated into the WWE's own *Smackdown* show.

In one of the final episodes, the *Tough Enough* contestants were forced to consume a large serving of pasta after undergoing vigorous exercise, which inevitably resulted in some of them throwing up. They were then sent to the ring, where they were verbally abused by WWE star Kurt Angle and obliged to compete in a squat thrust competition. With the participants suitably exhausted, the plan was that Angle - who won a gold medal in freestyle wrestling at the 1996 Olympics - would take on a number of them in a series of legitimate wrestling matches that he was expected to dominate and quickly win.

Angle first faced Chris Nawrocki, who had no wrestling experience and was completely knackered. Nawrocki was immediately taken down to the mat and pinned in 27 seconds. He was later hospitalised with a broken rib. Angle, adopting the role of class bully, then hollered, 'Who wants to get in the ring?' at the rest of the contestants, who were stood at ringside. Daniel Puder, a mixed martial arts fighter who was unbeaten in four contests at the time, raised his hand.

What followed was an object lesson in why pro wrestling became scripted in the first place. Angle immediately attempted to take Puder down to the mat but his efforts were blocked by the trained fighter. Angle persevered, backed his opponent into the corner and placed him in a front facelock, only for Puder to escape the hold. The former Olympian then went for a suplex. In the process, Puder managed to grab Angle's right arm and place it in a jiu-jitsu armlock known as a *kimura*.

Both competitors fell to the mat as Puder clung on to Angle's arm. Puder landed on his back but was in such a position that, had he chosen to do so, he could have cranked Angle's shoulder out of its socket. With the fight going exactly how WWE *hadn't* planned it, backstage officials panicked and, via the earpiece he was wearing, the referee was ordered to quickly count Puder down for three, even though he had evidently lifted his shoulders off the mat. (A second ref even tried to indicate as much.)

The match was called to a halt after 42 seconds and Angle was declared the winner via pinfall, despite the fact that he was trapped in a submission hold at the time. Even the live crowd recognised that Angle had been bailed out by the ref and responded with loud booing and a chant of 'bullshit'. Puder went on to win *Tough Enough* and a WWE contract, after which he was sent to WWE's training camp in Louisville, Kentucky. But his tenure with the company was short-lived: he was fired in September 2005 as a cost-cutting measure.

June Byers vs Mildred Burke

Atlanta, Georgia, August 1954

Female grapplers attempt to resolve title dispute with legitimate contest

The heyday of women's wrestling in the US, during the mid-20th century, can be credited to one man: Billy Wolfe. A former middleweight wrestler, on retiring from the ring he began to train women to wrestle at a gym in Kansas City. He went on to marry one of his students, Mildred Bliss, who adopted the pseudonym of Mildred Burke and won the women's world championship from Clara Mortenson in January 1937.

By 1949, Wolfe had built up a stable of 30 wrestlers, who he would hire out to other promoters for a percentage of the box office takings. It was a lucrative business. Wolfe was notorious for his womanising though and Burke left him in 1952. The split was both personal and professional: Burke was on her third reign as women's champion, meaning that Wolfe had lost control of the title that was at the centre of his booking agency. At first, Wolfe attempted, without success, to have Burke blacklisted from the profession by insisting that other promoters didn't employ her. The dispute was resolved, or so it seemed, when Wolfe sold his wrestling promotion and booking business to Burke for $30,000. He agreed to not have any involvement in the mat game for five years, a period that actually lasted for only a few months.

Wolfe restarted his booking agency and succeeded in taking many of the top women performers back under his wing. As a result, Burke's own enterprise went bankrupt and the receiver nominated Wolfe as administrator, leaving him in control of Burke's stable of wrestlers. Crucially, Burke was still in possession of the women's championship though. Wolfe responded by creating his own version of the title, which he awarded to his daughter-in-law June Byers, who won a 13-woman tournament in Baltimore in June 1953. But fans still considered Burke to be the 'legitimate' women's title-holder – which was significant because holding the title greatly increased a wrestler's ability to attract crowds and, hence, revenue.

It was agreed that the quarrel should be resolved by Burke and Byers facing each other in a best-of-three-falls unification match. Rather than the outcome being determined in advance by a promoter, as is typically the case in pro wrestling, this would be a genuine contest between the two title claimants. Burke began her career in 1935 by participating in 'shoot' (legitimate) matches at carnivals, where she would offer $25 to any man of a similar weight who could pin her within 10 minutes.

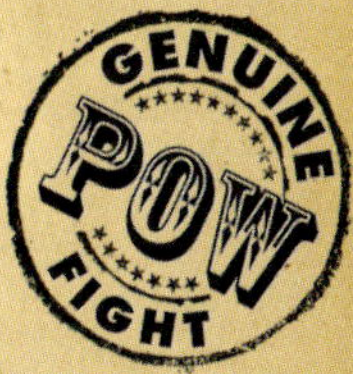

She had around 150 such fights, which she claimed to have never lost. So she was not overly concerned by the threat posed by Byers, even when she injured her knee shortly before the clash.

But Byers (who had been training with amateur wrestler Ruffy Silverstein) won the first fall when Burke submitted to a kneelock. Even after Burke conceded defeat, Byers didn't release the hold and dislocated her opponent's knee. In severe pain, Burke was unable to score an equaliser during the subsequent session. But she was a strong enough defensive wrestler that she was able to prevent Byers from winning the second fall that she needed to claim the title.

The stalemate continued for another 30 minutes until the state athletic commission stopped the match and ruled it a no-contest – a verdict that resolved nothing. Burke assumed she had retained the belt as she hadn't lost the required two falls but Wolfe claimed that Byers had won on points and most promoters across the US recognised Byers as the rightful champion. Burke continued to claim her version of the title – the WWWA championship – which she retained until her retirement the following year.

Steve Williams vs Bart Gunn

Anaheim, California, July 1998

Renowned hard man's WWF career ends after being pounded in legit scuffle

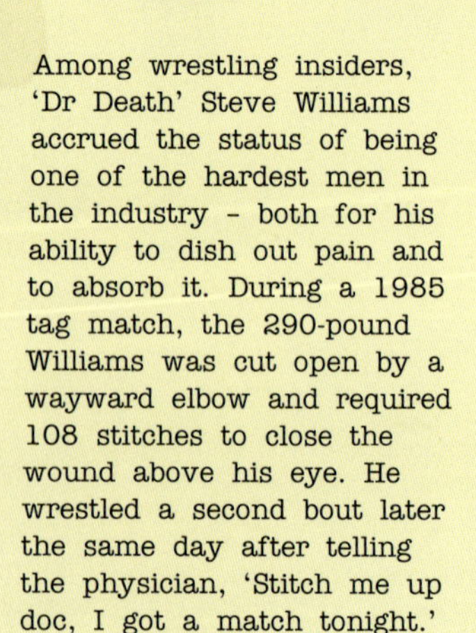

Among wrestling insiders, 'Dr Death' Steve Williams accrued the status of being one of the hardest men in the industry - both for his ability to dish out pain and to absorb it. During a 1985 tag match, the 290-pound Williams was cut open by a wayward elbow and required 108 stitches to close the wound above his eye. He wrestled a second bout later the same day after telling the physician, 'Stitch me up doc, I got a match tonight.'

When he joined the WWF in 1998, the company thought it had come up with the ideal vehicle to showcase what it considered to be his legitimate fighting credentials: a 16-man tournament, dubbed *Brawl for All*, in which participants wore outsize boxing gloves and were awarded points for landing punches and wrestling takedowns. The catch? None of the action was scripted. Instead, for the first time in its history, the WWF chose to promote a series of genuine punch-ups.

The WWF was confident that Williams would put in an impressive showing and, as a result, be able to main event shows against top star 'Stone Cold' Steve Austin. It didn't quite work out, though. Williams convincingly won his first fight (albeit by beating Pierre Ouellet, who was blind in one eye). He was then matched against mediocre tag team wrestler Bart Gunn in the quarter-finals. It was the beginning of the end of both men's WWF careers.

'Dr Death' dominated the first of the three, one-minute rounds and scored a takedown. Gunn regrouped in the second round and executed a takedown of his own that sent Williams sprawling under the bottom rope and tore his hamstring and buttocks - something that doesn't even sound possible. Despite the genuine violence that was taking place, the crowd found the contest tedious thanks to its clumsy brawling and lack of the choreographed exchanges they had been conditioned to expect. As such, when the bell rang for the final round, the two wrestlers were greeted by loud chants of 'boring!'

Williams was, by now, completely knackered, which again enabled Gunn to take him down to the mat, this time resulting in Williams' knee being dislocated. Back on his feet, 'Dr Death' was limping badly and unable to defend himself, which allowed Gunn to unload with a relentless series of punches that left Williams in a daze. The assault culminated with a ruinous left hook that knocked out Williams and dislocated his jaw.

The former amateur grappler was sidelined for months with his injuries and didn't return to WWF rings until January 1999. He was fired two months later after only a handful of forgettable appearances at the bottom of the bill. Gunn, meanwhile, went on to win the *Brawl for All* tournament after battering John 'Bradshaw' Layfield in the final. The WWF tried to play off his success by pitting him against comic boxing hero Eric 'Butterbean' Esch in a conclusion to the *Brawl for All* folly at *WrestleMania XV*. Contrary to the company's expectations, Gunn was knocked out in 35 seconds, which promptly marked the end of his WWF career.

Dirt Bike Kid vs Great Sasuke

Yahaba, Japan, July 1999

Forthright Brit flies to Japan, disrespects promoter, gets beaten up, flies home

When British wrestler Jason Harrison arrived in Japan in July 1999, it was supposed to have been the highpoint of his career. For almost five years as the motocross outfit-clad Dirt Bike Kid, he had been attempting to establish himself by trawling the poorly-paid UK circuit, creating and awarding himself the European junior heavyweight championship, and promoting a trio of shows in Walthamstow, London, on which he faced imported stars such as Sabu and Mikey Whipwreck. Having found little success in his home country, the opportunity to appear on a Japanese tour for Michinoku Pro Wrestling signified considerable progress.

Dirt Bike was to be a participant in a five-week long masked man league, the loser of which would be forced to reveal their identity. Although he never donned a wrestling mask in the UK, he was required to do so by Michinoku throughout the tournament. But Harrison had other ideas.

Before the tour even started, the Brit grappler hadn't endeared himself to his Japanese hosts. He had refused to pose for promotional photos and threatened to pull out of the tournament due to the modest remuneration (he would earn the equivalent of just £75 per match). Despite these initial snags, Harrison flew to Japan as arranged for the tour's first show on 17 July, on which he would face Michinoku Pro's boss and top star the Great Sasuke.

Prior to the match, Sasuke (real name Masanori Murakawa) was curiously aloof and spent very little time discussing with Harrison the exchanges they would perform – contrary to how wrestling matches are usually put together. While there was a sense of underlying tension between the two, no one was quite prepared for what happened next.

Once in the ring, Dirt Bike Kid waited for his name to be announced by the MC. At which point, he removed his mask – the very aspect of his costume that justified his slot in the tournament in the first place – and held it

aloft. He then flung it to the mat, while Sasuke looked on dispassionately (not difficult given that he was wearing a mask himself). After the bell rang and the match commenced, Sasuke conspicuously offered no offence whatsoever, as Dirt Bike performed a series of slams and dives.

But when he went for a splash off the top rope, Sasuke rolled out of the way and attacked Harrison with a vengeance. In violent contrast to DBK's pulled punches, he unleashed 18 full-force kicks to his foe's upper body and head, before locking in a painful neck crank that legitimately forced Harrison to submit. As Dirt Bike rolled on the mat in obvious discomfort, Sasuke celebrated his victory by performing a cartwheel in front of his vanquished opponent. The hapless Brit was subsequently whisked to the local hospital, where he was diagnosed with broken cartilage on the right side of his chest.

In the wrestlers' hotel the following morning, Harrison ate his breakfast alone, nursing both bruised ribs and a bruised ego. Sasuke entered the room and approached his table. He said simply, 'You go home on Saturday.' After just a single bout for Michinoku Pro, Harrison was fired and sent back to the UK. He never worked for the company again and retired from wrestling the following year. Great Sasuke, meanwhile, went on to be elected as a local councillor in Morioka, northern Japan, and continued to wear his wrestling mask while in office.

Earthquake vs Koji Kitao

Kobe, Japan, April 1991

Grumpy Japanese star refuses to adhere to script and attacks referee

When John 'Earthquake' Tenta faced Koji Kitao at the Tokyo Dome on 30 March 1991, the match was keenly anticipated by Japanese fans as both had been stars in sumo. Despite the lacklustre action, which quickly ended when 'Quake pinned Kitao after a sit-down splash, the bout garnered the biggest response of the night from fans in the stadium.

But Kitao was upset at being defeated in such a decisive manner and the bout was littered with numerous shoddy exchanges. When a rematch took place two days later in Kobe, Kitao was offended at again having to lose and, in protest, was determinedly uncooperative in the ring. The deceptively powerful Tenta attempted to hold the bout together by manhandling his sulky opponent - at one point, he even managed the impressive feat of suplexing him without cooperation.

After a few minutes, things fell apart completely when Kitao attempted to poke Earthquake in the eyes, and the two wrestlers simply stood in the centre of the ring yelling at one another. The referee finally brought an end to the mess when he disqualified Kitao for kicking him to the mat. The disgruntled grappler then left the ring, grabbed the microphone and yelled at Tenta, 'You're just a monkey in this fake wrestling circus,' which, as insults go, is at least pretty creative.

Kitao didn't fare much better at mixed martial arts: at UFC IX in May 1996, it took Mark Hall - a man half his size - all of 47 seconds to beat him with a brutal onslaught of punches to the head.

Midnight Express vs Rock 'n' Roll Express

Beckley, West Virginia, May 1987

Promotion sued for $6.3 million after wrestler leaps into crowd and attacks fan

Bobby Eaton and Stan Lane, collectively the Midnight Express, were one of the most hated tag teams in wrestling during their late-1980s heyday, not least thanks to the antics of tennis racquet-wielding manager Jim Cornette, who had an unrivalled ability to anger fans. Their main event against the Rock 'n' Roll Express – Ricky Morton and Robert Gibson – at the Raleigh County Armory in May 1987 demonstrated that Cornette was, at times, almost *too* effective in his role.

The audience was particularly rowdy that night and, after Cornette smacked Morton with his racquet, one drunken fan vaulted over the rail in a bid to attack the manager. The over-enthusiastic spectator was carried out of the venue by security but both teams sensed that the audience was becoming dangerously riled and the match was quickly wrapped up, with the Rock 'n' Roll Express gaining the victory.

While the Midnights were waiting to be escorted back to the dressing room by security, a fan hurled a wooden aisle marker into the ring, which hit Eaton in the neck and shoulder. Lane leapt into the crowd and punched the fan he thought was responsible – a 5ft 6in tall 62-year-old called Roy Massey – in the face, fracturing the orbit of his left eye and other facial bones (he was hospitalised for eight days). Massey was then escorted backstage, where he thought he would be given an apology. Instead, Cornette unleashed a tirade of abuse and called him a 'drunken hillbilly' who 'ought to be kicked off the face of the earth'.

Massey responded to the physical assault by filing a $6.3 million suit seeking to recover damages for personal injuries. It was never clearly established who actually threw the marker: some witnesses testified that Massey was responsible, while others said that a teenager threw the object and then fled the arena. The case was finally settled out of court in 1991 and Massey received $600,000 from the promoter's insurance company.

Perry Saturn vs Mike Bell

Long Island, New York, May 2001

Veteran wrestler forced to become smitten with mop as punishment for battering unsuspecting fall guy

The key to pro wrestling is that wrestlers create the illusion of violence by cooperating with one another in the ring. Indeed, many moves - such as the vertical suplex - are impossible if the victim of the manoeuvre doesn't assist with its execution. Such cooperation broke down completely during a televised WWF match between former WCW tag champion Perry Saturn and preliminary

wrestler Mike Bell, an experienced journeyman (he was one of John Cena's original trainers) who had worked intermittently as 'enhancement talent' for the WWF since 1992 and was desperate to become a full-time member of the troupe.

After the two exchanged a series of holds and reversals, Bell threw Saturn into the ropes and then employed a hiptoss, in which your opponent does a mid-air somersault before, in theory, landing flat on their back. Saturn didn't fully rotate though and instead landed on his shoulder and head, spraining his neck. Bell then attempted an armdrag and, again, Saturn landed awkwardly.

Furious at what he considered to be Bell's incompetence, and further enraged when he lost his balance and fell over when he attempted a kick, Saturn hit Bell with full-force punches and violently threw him from the ring to the floor, where the unfortunate hopeful landed on his head (and could have easily broken his neck). Curiously, Saturn asked Bell if he was OK before he continued the assault by driving him viciously into the steel ring steps.

Back in the squared circle, Saturn hooked Bell's legs under the top turnbuckle and suspended him upside-down in the corner (a move known as the tree of woe), which enabled Saturn to apply a ferocious chinlock. In a bid to protect Bell from further damage, Saturn's manager Terri Runnels ran around the ring and hugged her charge, forcing him to release the defenceless Bell. Satisfied that he had given Bell a sufficient beating, Saturn then returned to delivering worked holds - Bell, to his credit, cooperated with a suplex and even kicked out after a two-count. Saturn finally put Bell out of his misery by going to the planned finish of a sidekick followed by a swinging cradle suplex.

If Saturn was employed in any other profession, he would surely have been fired (and possibly even arrested) for his actions. But this being pro wrestling, his punishment took a more creative bent: he had to play the role of someone who had fallen in love with a mop with a face painted on it, which he named 'Moppy'. As the storyline developed, Runnels told Saturn that he had to choose between her or the cleaning implement. Saturn opted for the latter, which compelled Runnels to leave Saturn for rival wrestler Raven (who, ironically, had held the WCW tag titles with Saturn). During an episode of *Raw* in September 2001, Raven kidnapped the mop, strapped it to a length of wood, gaffer taped its mouth and fed it into a wood chipper.

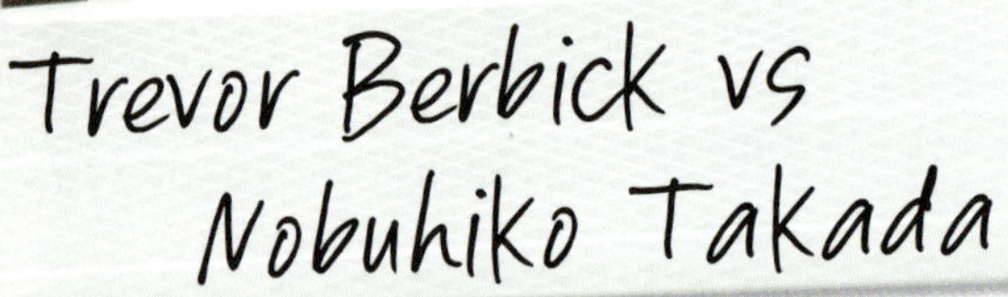

Trevor Berbick vs Nobuhiko Takada

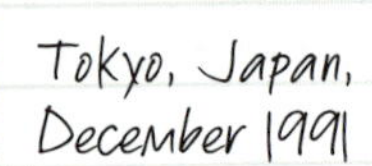

Tokyo, Japan, December 1991

Boxer vs wrestler face-off descends into farce when former heavyweight champ flees ring

Pro wrestling has long blurred the line between fiction and reality. Never was that more apparent than in Japan's 'shoot style' promotions, which flourished from the mid-1980s to the mid-1990s. The idea was to present pro wrestling as a sport, without the accoutrements of the histrionic American style. The UWFI was the last of such outfits to garner significant success. Its roster of fighters would throw kicks and punches at near-full force but, while the company often proclaimed that its matches were genuine sporting contests, the results were still predetermined.

Trevor Berbick must have thought it would be an easy payday. The former WBC world heavyweight boxing champion (he lost the title to Mike Tyson in 1986) was offered 10 per cent of the box office receipts to face UWFI's top star Nobuhiko Takada in the main event of a show that would take place in an 11,000-capacity arena – at the time, the biggest show the grap group had ever promoted.

Berbick was assured that his meeting with Takada would be an 'exhibition' – that is, it would be based on the two fighters cooperating with one another as opposed to having an authentic confrontation. But in the week before the bout, Berbick watched videos of some of Takada's previous fights and became gravely concerned about the force of his leg kicks, worrying that a powerful kick to his knee could hinder his boxing career. He ordered his lawyers to negotiate new rules for the match that banned Takada from throwing kicks below the waist.

The dispute over the rules was never resolved and, immediately before the contest, Berbick demanded an additional $5,000 in cash before he would enter the ring. What followed was a farcical spectacle that satisfied neither fans of pro wrestling nor aficionados of genuine fisticuffs. Takada opened the match by throwing a roundhouse kick at Berbick's leg. Aggrieved, the boxer dropped his guard and complained to the referee. The crowd was unimpressed and started to boo.

The fighters squared up to each another for a second time and Takada booted Berbick in the leg. The boxer (who beat a past-his-prime Muhammad Ali in Ali's last fight in 1981) again appealed to the ref, to no avail. Takada continued the onslaught and staggered his opponent with a kick to the knee, followed by further kicks to the leg. Panicking, Berbick shuffled towards the edge of the ring and wrapped his arm over the top rope. This resulted in a comical interlude in which the referee tried to prise Berbick from the ropes, while Takada simultaneously threw more leg strikes at him.

Berbick then backed into the corner, at which point the referee began yelling, 'Fight! Fight!' at him. It did no good and Berbick again dropped his guard, allowing Takada to punt his stationary target in the head, before again targeting Berbick's left hamstring. When another kick hit his left knee, Berbick decided he'd had enough and, less than three minutes into the scrap and having mounted no offence whatsoever, he leapt out of the ring into the press section. From a kneeling position he yelled, 'Fuck you! That ain't the rules!' The bell rang and Takada was declared the winner, prompting the irate audience to throw rubbish at the ring and chant 'coward!' at Berbick.

Despite his posturing of being a fearsome martial artist, Takada subsequently compiled a lacklustre record in Pride, a Japanese version of the Ultimate Fighting Championship. In 2004, having retired from legitimate fighting, he became the president of short-lived wrestling group Hustle, a WWE-style league based around over-the-top caricatures and comedy. When he made his return to the ring as a professional wrestler, he was billed as a cyborg called The Esperanza.

Lex Luger vs Bruiser Brody

Lakeland, Florida, January 1987

Distraught rookie abandons match as opponent decides to stop cooperating

IMPROMPTU FINISH

Before he became a star in WCW and the WWF, Lex Luger was just another novice grappler with a well-defined physique and little else. He began his career in the small-time Florida territory, which is where he first faced Bruiser Brody, whose wildman appearance was matched by his often uncooperative demeanour. During the first few contests between the two, the inexperienced Luger failed to sell Brody's strikes and holds to the veteran's satisfaction. When they again faced one another in a cage match in January 1987, Brody decided to forcefully demonstrate to Luger the flaws in his methodology.

The beginning of the encounter was orthodox enough, with the two cooperating in the exchange of headlocks, armbars and punches. Brody even allowed Luger to throw him into the cage. But after four minutes of back-and-forth action, Brody stopped participating in the match. When Luger unleashed a series of punches and shoulder blocks, Brody simply stood in the corner of the ring, staring at him. Luger increased the intensity of his blows but Brody continued to just glare at the disconcerted rookie.

Whatever the genuine drama that was unfolding inside the ring, the spectacle was a tedious one for the audience, who began to boo. Luger looked to the referee for instructions, who advised him to continue the bout as planned. Brody then decided to toy with his opponent further by taking Luger down to the mat and kneeling on him, before placing him in a front facelock. By now, Luger thought he was about to receive a legitimate battering and brought the match to an impromptu conclusion by throwing the referee to the canvas in order to be disqualified. Luger promptly clambered over the top of the cage, headed backstage, gathered his belongings and left the venue before Brody even made it back to the dressing room.

Steve Ray vs Steve Williams New York, May 1991

Unhinged promoter dishes out bonus payment to wrestler for breaking opponent's nose

Numerous wrestling promotions have used the initials UWF – but none were so low-rent as the Universal Wrestling Federation, which was founded in 1990 by the notoriously unscrupulous Herb Abrams and was based around 1980s stars such as Paul Orndorff, Don Muraco and Bob Orton Jr. When the volatile Abrams wrongly suspected wrestler 'Wild Thing' Steve Ray of having an affair with his wife, he took the sort of idiosyncratic approach to addressing the situation that only a particularly devious wrestling promoter could.

Without giving anything away to Ray, Abrams booked him to face 'Dr Death' Steve Williams in a match that took place in New York's Hotel Pennsylvania. Abrams then paid Williams an extra $100 (which says a lot about the UWF's pay scale) to break Ray's nose during the bout. 'Dr Death' was happy to oblige and booted his unfortunate opponent in the face, shattering his conk. Abrams scuttled into the ring and goaded Ray after he'd been pinned, only for Ray to take a wild swing at him. The bout later aired in its entirety on the UWF's cable TV show.

Abrams died five years later, at the age of 41, in suitably wacky circumstances. Manhattan police had been alerted to a disturbance in a high-rise office. On arrival, they discovered that Abrams – who was out of his gourd on cocaine – was naked, slathered in baby oil and demolishing his office with a baseball bat. He was promptly arrested and died around 90 minutes later as the result of a massive heart attack.

Wendi Richter vs The Spider

New York, November 1985

Women's champion storms out of WWF after contract dispute ends with unscripted title change

For much of the latter part of the 20th century, American women's wrestling was synonymous with Lillian 'Fabulous Moolah' Ellison. She first won a version of the world women's championship in September 1956 and dominated the title for much of the next 30 years (not least due to her parallel role at the time as the leading booking agent for female wrestlers across North America).

Despite the fact that Moolah's matches had been tedious and hackneyed for decades, huge mainstream attention beckoned when the WWF began to recognise Moolah as its own women's champion, after she sold the company the rights to the belt in 1983. Wendi Richter, a protégé of Moolah's, was subsequently paired up with then-hugely popular singer Cyndi Lauper, who acted as Richter's manager during high-profile matches in 1984-85, as part of a cross-promotion dubbed the Rock 'n' Wrestling Connection. Richter ('150 pounds of twisted steel and sex appeal') toppled Moolah, by then in her early sixties, for the women's title in a July 1984 match that was broadcast live on MTV. Billed as ***The Brawl to End it All***, the bout was atrocious. Yet it still ranks as one of the most widely viewed wrestling matches in the history of US cable television.

During her second reign as champion in 1985, Richter began to demand greater remuneration, believing that she had been underpaid for her appearance at the first ***WrestleMania*** (which was headlined by a match involving Mr T) and threatened to quit the promotion while still champion. As a result, WWF boss Vince McMahon decided to swindle Richter out of the women's title. At a show in Madison Square Garden, Richter went to the ring expecting to retain her title against masked wrestler The Spider, a character usually played by Penny Mitchell. Only on this occasion, it was Moolah wearing the costume. Given the size and age difference between Moolah and Mitchell, it wasn't difficult to work out who was under the disguise – ringside fans even chanted 'Moolah' at the start of the match.

After almost seven minutes of mediocre wrestling, The Spider broke from the script and attempted to forcibly pin Richter's shoulders to the mat for a three-count. Richter clearly kicked out at one but the referee, who had been tipped off about the deception, counted to three anyway. The bell rang to signify the end of the bout, although the ref didn't raise either woman's hand in victory. A puzzled Richter attempted to continue the match, even as the MC entered the ring: she unmasked Moolah, executed a sloppy-looking backbreaker (Moolah had stopped cooperating by this point) and attempted a pinfall of her own, which the referee refused to count.

When Moolah was announced as the new champion, Richter snatched the title belt and attempted to clobber her with it, forcing Moolah to retreat backstage. Richter dropped the championship to the mat in disgust and, infuriated, stormed to the dressing room, grabbed her belongings and took a cab to the airport, without even changing out of her wrestling gear. She never worked for the WWF again.

MAN-MACHINE
ABSURD COSTUME
OVERZEALOUS FANS
SURREAL
INJURY
BLOOD
勝利

CHAPTER 7:
CALL THAT A WRESTLER?
ANIMAL
Comedy
MR DANGER
HITMAN
DOOMED CONCEPT

Mitsuhiro Matsunaga vs an alligator

BLOOD

DOOMED CONCEPT

ANIMAL

Tokyo, Japan, September 1998

Deathmatch whiz forced to wrestle reptile as forfeit for losing championship

Japanese hardcore wrestler Mitsuhiro Matsunaga wasn't nicknamed 'Mr Danger' for nothing. The deathmatch specialist was a veteran of bouts that invariably entailed the use of an arsenal of flesh-shredding implements and he rarely ended a match without being covered in blood. In a bid not so much to push as to bludgeon the boundaries of pro wrestling, he pioneered diving off balconies, once had his head set on fire by nemesis Mr Pogo and took part in matches in which he was bitten by piranhas and stung by scorpions.

In September 1998, he agreed to take part in what sounded as if it could be his most dangerous match yet. He was scheduled to defend his Big Japan Pro Wrestling deathmatch championship against Satoru Shiga (who used the ring name Shadow WX). As an additional forfeit, the loser would then have to face an alligator in a 'coffin deathmatch'. Perhaps expecting to see a wrestler confront a vicious creature hungry for human flesh, fans keenly anticipated the show's climax.

The contest between Matsunaga and Shiga was built around many of Big Japan's familiar motifs. After brawling into the foyer, 'Mr Danger' suplexed Shadow through a number of fluorescent light tubes attached to a large board, which was balanced across a staircase. The die-hard Big Japan fans crowded around the two wrestlers, apparently unconcerned by the risk of being hit by shattering glass, as they bellowed Matsunaga's name.

For the bout's subsequent set piece, WX powerbombed the long-suffering Matsunaga off a stage through a pair of barbed wire and light tube-ensconced boards that were resting on two chairs (Shiga lost his footing and Matsunaga almost landed face-first). Back in the ring, Shadow WX, perplexingly, broke a light tube over his own head, before powerslamming Matsunaga on to a bed of nails for the pinfall.

It was a bad night for Matsunaga: he was bleeding profusely, had lost his deathmatch championship and now had to attempt to contest some sort of wrestling match with a live alligator. It didn't go well. The alligator was brought to the ring in a large crate and netting was placed over the ropes to prevent it from escaping. 'Mr Danger' flipped the crate and hesitantly lifted it up to reveal that, far from being the man-eating monster that fans were anticipating, the alligator was only about four feet long and clearly posed no threat to the wrestler whatsoever. Indeed, it scurried to the edge of the ring and then stubbornly stayed put.

Matsunaga grabbed the reptile by the tail and placed it in a coffin in the centre of the ring. He hovered his foot in front of the docile creature in a vain attempt to coerce it into attacking him but the 'gator, sensibly, wasn't interested and remained motionless. Matsunaga discussed what to do with the referee but it was abundantly clear that what had been built up as an attraction in which 'Mr Danger' really would live up to his nickname was destined for unconditional failure. After not even the semblance of any kind of action, the exasperated grappler put the lid on the casket to win the match and prove conclusively that you simply can't teach an alligator to wrestle.

Hulk Hogan & Dennis Rodman vs Dallas Page & Karl Malone

San Diego, California, July 1998

Wasted NBA star falls asleep during pay-per-view main event

When WCW signed basketball bad boy Dennis Rodman to appear in the main event of *Bash at the Beach*, the company must have considered that Rodman's $750,000 asking price would be money well spent. Sure, he wasn't a trained wrestler - but at 6ft 6in tall and boasting a toned physique and a gallery of tattoos, he did at least look the part. The idea was that the curiosity of seeing a mainstream sports star wrestle would draw new viewers and attract attention from the mainstream press. And it worked: his tag team contest at the pay-per-view event generated a gross revenue of almost $7 million and was covered by publications such as *USA Today* and *Sports Illustrated.*

Although the match was a financial triumph, artistically it was a disaster. The NBA star vanished during the day of the show and, when he belatedly arrived at San Diego's Cox Arena in no condition to perform, company officials were relieved that he was there at all and sent him to the ring anyway. 'Rodzilla' had been up all night and was barely capable of walking, let alone pulling off anything that resembled a wrestling match.

The near 25-minute bout was characterised by two things: stalling and Rodman falling over. While he was incapable of executing even the most basic grappling holds, he proved to be an expert in losing his balance and unintentionally falling to the mat in a heap. As Hogan covered for him in the ring (the 'Hulkster' won the bout for his team when he pinned Page), at one point Rodders even rested his head on the turnbuckle and appeared to take a nap half-way through the fight. He later claimed that he had been defrauded in contract negotiations and sued WCW for $550,000.

Comedy

Yatchan & Shoichi Ichimiya vs Seiya Morohashi & Tanomusaku Toba

Tokyo, Japan, January 2005

Japanese duo takes on macaque monkey in tag team championship match

ANIMAL

What low-budget Japanese promotion Dramatic Dream Team lacks in star power it compensates for with sheer, unadulterated lunacy. Hence this contest, which featured a denim-clad macaque monkey called Yatchan who, with tag partner Shoichi Ichimiya, was putting in a challenge for the company's tag team titles. The belts were suspended above a ladder in the centre of the ring: whoever was able to climb up and grab them first would win the match and the championship. As an added incentive, a large bunch of bananas was also hung next to the titles.

Throughout the duration of the shambolic contest, Yatchan wisely paid no attention to the other wrestlers whatsoever. He wasn't even that interested in the bananas. Indeed, whenever his karate gi-wearing handler placed him on the ladder in the vain hope that he would make a grab for the dangling championship gold, the primate instead vaulted across the ring. Clearly, no one had explained the rules to him.

Morohashi began to climb the ladder himself, only to be thwarted by the monkey's partner Ichimiya, who stopped his progress by pulling down his wrestling tights and shoving a banana in the crack of his arse. Toba then attempted to involve the baffled ape in the contest by throwing obviously pulled punches at him, followed by a simulated back suplex. The nonsense was concluded when Morohashi cornered the ape, allowing his partner to climb the ladder and seize the championship belts. The monkey played it cool and appeared to be wholly indifferent to the loss.

Shockwave the Robot vs Earl Cooter

Bellmore, New York, May 2009

Crazed hillbilly attempts to shut down robot by pouring beer over it

ABSURD COSTUME

What do you do if you're a journeyman wrestler with eight years' experience but still haven't had the career break you're looking for? Reinvent yourself as 'the world's only breakdancing wrestling robot'. Which is what Shockwave the Robot – he won't reveal his real name – did in 2006, a move that resulted in bookings across the US, Canada and Japan.

Any wrestling match that involves a man clad in a silver body suit, while pretending to be an automaton, is going to be peculiar. But this particular scrap was made odder still when said robot was matched against a trailer park-dwelling hick named Earl Cooter who claimed to be from 'Stinkwater, Tennessee'. This clash of redneck and robot began when Cooter – clad in his trademark trucker hat, stained vest and impossibly ripped jeans – challenged Shockwave to a dance-off. Cooter then ran around the ring as if attempting an impression of a chicken suffering a particularly sustained heart attack, before Shockwave demonstrated his breakdancing skills. Of course, dancing doesn't come naturally to robots. 'I was horrible when I first started,' admits Shockwave. 'I don't have that good a rhythm. It took at least four or five months for me to have the moves down pretty good.'

Enraged by Shockwave's body popping, Cooter attacked the dancing droid, only for Shockwave to retaliate by shooting him in the face with the confetti blaster attached to his right arm, after which the match officially began. Shockwave started proceedings by placing Cooter ('Mess with me and you mess with the whole trailer park') in a simple hammerlock. In mock agony, the hillbilly screamed, 'Aaargh, get him off me!' as if he was being mauled by the Terminator itself.

MAN-MACHINE

The denouement began as Cooter rolled out of the ring and headed to the ice box he'd earlier placed at ringside. He pulled a bottle of beer from it and poured its contents over Shockwave's back. 'I was dying of laughter,' says Shockwave. 'I'd told him, "Look, I just got this suit done. Try not to splash that much beer on it." So he shook this beer up and poured it all over me.' Lager and circuitry don't really mix and the robot, inevitably, short-circuited. The man-machine broke down in the middle of the ring, where he slumped over, seemingly unable to move.

In on the joke, the crowd chanted 'reboot!' while the referee told Cooter in no uncertain terms that he would be disqualified if he was unable to repair Shockwave. Cooter retrieved a spanner that, handily, he kept in the ice box along with his beers and attempted to fix the knackered android. At first, he was only able to get Shockwave's left hand working - which he used to crush Cooter's balls, causing the redneck wrestler to scream in agony. Cooter then gave up on his impromptu robotic repair and decided to just charge at the contraption instead. Shockwave suddenly sprang back to life and hit Cooter with a drop toe-hold, a spinning heel kick and a top-rope huracanrana, after which he secured the pinfall. Had he never heard of the Three Laws of Robotics?

Piza Michinoku & Antonio Honda vs Yoshihiko & Danshoku Dino

Tokyo, Japan, April 2009

Wrestler wins tag match despite partner - an inflatable sex doll - being 'killed' during bout

Pro wrestling has always been populated by a curious parade of freaks. But deeming the usual array of wrestling stereotypes to be passé, Japanese grap crew Dramatic Dream Team decided the next logical step was to treat inanimate objects as sentient combatants. To wit, Yoshihiko: a blow-up sex doll with a felt tipped-on goatee and full-sleeve tattoos, designed to resemble WWE star The Undertaker. The other participants in Yoshihiko's matches naturally played it completely straight, as if the doll was a genuine wrestler, not just an inflatable novelty item.

Sensibly, Dino started this match for his team after purporting to discuss tactics with his partner. When he then tagged in the doll, Honda locked up with it in a test of strength, before he positioned Yoshihiko to make it appear as if it was putting him in a side headlock. Honda eventually summoned the energy for a comeback, which culminated in a powerful kneedrop to Yoshihiko's head that caused it to burst. Dino reacted as if his tag partner had been fatally wounded and looked on aghast as the doll was carefully carried backstage to receive emergency medical attention.

Dino was left to battle the two villains alone for a few minutes, after which the lights dimmed and a pair of stage hands triumphantly carried a new incarnation of Yoshihiko to the ring, this time modified to resemble mist-spewing Japanese wrestler the Great Muta. The heel wrestlers somehow managed to make out that the inflatable doll was dominating them with flying headscissors and moonsaults. The doll then spat green mist into Honda's face, allowing the 'blinded' wrestler to be pinned by Dino (who had earlier attempted to secure a submission victory over Honda by kissing him passionately on the lips). A thrilled Dino jubilantly paraded around the ring – wrestling sex doll in hand – to celebrate his victory.

Electric Heater vs Ladder

Tokyo, Japan, March 2006

Wrestling finally eats itself as human grapplers are replaced by inanimate objects

Wrestling doesn't get much more avant-garde - or ridiculous - than this. In lieu of the traditional approach of pitting two men (or women) against one another, this bout from lo-fi independent chancers Ishi Summit pitted a small stepladder against a **kotatsu**, a Japanese heater in the form of a low wooden table covered by a heavy blanket. Handily, the blanket hid all four sides of the device, thus enabling someone to crouch beneath it. The ladder, alas, had no such advantage.

While the ladder stood impassively in the centre of the mat, the heater could be seen to quiver slightly, as if to build up momentum. As the excitable spectators began a chant of '**Kotatsu**!' the plucky heater lurched forward and toppled its otherwise static opponent. With the crowd continuing to shout encouragement, the winter warmer crawled atop its felled adversary and - much to the delight of the hipster audience - the referee counted the pinfall, finally resolving the classic pub argument of what would win a fight between a small ladder and a space heater.

Could this match have been a knowing satire of the proliferation of household items now employed in professional wrestling matches, a wry commentary on how far removed the modern entertainment form has become from its sports-based roots? Or was it just a load of old nonsense? Whatever the case, the rest of the wrestling industry remained distinctly unimpressed: a reporter for respected Japanese magazine *Weekly Pro Wrestling* later said of the contest, 'This is disgusting and bullshit.'

Bret Hart vs Tom Magee

Rochester, New York, October 1986

'Hitman' fools WWF boss into thinking he's found the next Hulk Hogan

DOOMED CONCEPT

On paper, Winnipeg native Tom Magee was the ideal candidate to join the ranks of 1980s WWF. He was 6ft 5in tall, acrobatic, boasted a bodybuilder's physique, and had a legitimate athletics background that included placing in the top five of the World's Strongest Man contest in 1982, 1983 and 1985. On the down side, he had no charisma whatsoever and was wholly incapable of working even a basic match.

None of which was apparent during his WWF try-out, in which he pinned future WWF champion Bret 'Hitman' Hart – despite Hart's protestations. Hart only agreed to lose the confrontation after WWF boss Vince McMahon assured him that it would never air on television.

Magee had been trained by Bret's father Stu, an old-time wrestler who founded a promotion named Stampede Wrestling, based in Calgary, Canada. Despite this, Bret had little faith in his inexperienced opponent. In his detailed autobiography *Hitman*, Hart recounts how he told Magee to only give him his three best moves and that he'd take care of everything else in the ring, although he still struggled to ensure that Magee was in the correct position for each manoeuvre. But it worked and, with his enthusiastic bump-taking, the 'Hitman' did such a convincing job of carrying his useless opponent to a decent-looking encounter that McMahon - who was watching on a backstage monitor - hollered that, in Magee, he had found his next champion. The WWF chief was convinced that he had discovered the successor to Hulk Hogan.

The reality was somewhat different. After Magee was subsequently signed by the WWF, he was given the nickname of 'MegaMan' and sent to work on the WWF's 'C' tour - minor, untelevised shows in small arenas - against journeyman wrestler Terry Gibbs. The idea was that he would gain the requisite in-ring experience before receiving a huge promotional push. But, without a regular opponent of Hart's calibre, Magee's complete lack of ability was quickly exposed. However hard Gibbs tried each night, the two still had the worst match on every show.

Magee began his matches by performing a 360 degree flip from the top rope, something that quickly proved to be the lone highlight of the bouts. His offence was so wooden that he might as well have been carved from mahogany and his hokey attempts at executing the backbreaker resulted in one of the phoniest-looking finishers ever conceived. Hart later said that Magee couldn't walk across the ring without tripping and, during one match with Gibbs that was taped for *Wrestling Challenge* (one of Magee's few WWF television appearances), even the WWF's own commentator referred to him as a 'musclehead'.

By mid-1987, the company had given up on him and, far from supplanting Hulk Hogan, Magee only ever wrestled again for the WWF on a handful of occasions. He went on to work briefly for All Japan Pro Wrestling, although he showed no signs of improvement: his April 1988 encounter for the promotion against Hiroshi Wajima was widely considered one of the decade's worst bouts. Indeed, his meeting with Bret Hart remains his solitary good match.

Mecha Mummy vs Mokujin Ken

Philadelphia, Pennsylvania, February 2001

Man clad in cardboard box faces robotic Egyptian mummy under 'industrial revolution street fight' rules

'The following match is not for the faint of heart,' intoned the ring announcer, ominously. 'But we will find out what happens when tree meets mummy.' As the frenzied guitar widdling of Mokujin Ken's entrance theme kicked in, the spectators in Philadelphia's New Alhambra Arena were met with the vista of a man ambling towards the ring dressed as a character from the videogame series *Tekken*. A character that was purported to be a 2,000-year-old kung fu training dummy that comes to life in the presence of powerful evil. From a distance, it looked like someone struggling to escape from an enormous cardboard box while sporting a brown paper bag on their head.

The walking box was soon followed by a bloke who had adopted the only slightly-less-absurd guise of an Egyptian mummy/robot hybrid, replete with outsize 'mechanised fist' on one hand and a three-feet long plastic drill attachment on the other.

It quickly became apparent that Mokujin Ken's costume left him incapable of entering the ring, meaning that the match – which was promoted by local outfit Chikara – was declared an 'industrial revolution street fight'. What this meant in practice was that the competitors waddled around the ringside area exchanging slow-motion right hooks. In between blows, Mokujin busied himself by randomly waggling his arms about and ensuring that his headwear didn't fall off.

As fans began an ironic chant of, 'This is awesome!' Mummy ascended to the arena's balcony, from where he flung his detachable mecha-fist at Mokujin's head. He followed up by supposedly impaling his disorientated opponent with his super-sized drill. With Mokujin flat on his back at the top of the walkway and apparently defenceless, Mecha Mummy continued the drill-based assault until the referee called a halt to the B-movie brutality and declared the electronic Egyptian the winner by TKO.

Invisible Mysterio vs Choun Shiryu

Tokyo, Japan, August 2007

Ill-fated mat man loses bout to opponent only he and the referee can see

SURREAL

It was once said that Ric Flair could have a decent match with a broomstick. But was he capable of having a worthwhile fight with himself? That was the task of Japanese wrestler Choun Shiryu when he faced Invisible Mysterio – an imaginary grappler seemingly visible only to his opponent and the referee – on a show promoted by indie league Dramatic Dream Team.

Choun Shiryu locked up with Mysterio to begin the bout and placed his unseen adversary in an armlock (that is, he approximated the movements he would make if he was performing such a move on a genuine opponent). Mysterio reversed the hold as the crowd collectively went 'ooooh!' appreciatively.

The 'two' grapplers exchanged punches (which made Shiryu look as if he was having some form of mental breakdown), with Mysterio's final blow sending Shiryu spinning across the ring. Shiryu retorted with a bodyslam and a series of headbutts, only for Mysterio to suplex him off the top rope – which meant that Shiryu had to climb to the top turnbuckle and somersault off it on to the empty mat below.

After almost 10 minutes of imaginary back-and-forth action, the match culminated with Shiryu attempting to execute a German suplex, only for his non-existent opponent to reverse the move and then score the winning three-count. Magnanimously, Shiryu raised his opponent's hand after losing the match to him. A relative of Mysterio's, another invisible wrestler named Arnold Sukesukejaneka, later went on to find success as a four-time holder of the company's ironman heavyweight championship.

Terrible Ted vs Bunny Dunlop

Toronto, Canada, January 1959

Wrestling bear escapes into crowd after being goaded by ringside fan

Where the Roman Empire pitted Christians against lions, America of the 1950s-1970s matched wrestlers against bears. The animals were trained to stand on their hind legs and playfully push their human opponents around the ring. One of the most renowned wrestling bears of the era was Terrible Ted, a 400lb black bear from the Gaspé Peninsula in Quebec. He was a popular novelty act who was used to embellish cards in between the more serious matches.

One of his early main events was against Bunny Dunlop in Toronto's Maple Leaf Gardens. Dunlop usually worked as a referee and had officiated Ted's previous match at the arena. During the bout, Dunlop had lost his temper with the animal and kicked him, which prompted Ted to attempt to maul his antagonist. This January 1959 contest was billed as a grudge match in which Dunlop would attempt to gain his revenge.

Dunlop entered the ring first, took off his jacket and stood in the corner awaiting his hirsute opponent. Ted was attached to a long chain and led to the ring by his owner Ted Garner. As the creature clambered up the steps into the ring, a fan ran up to Terrible Ted and starting poking him. Ted swiped at the irritant with his paw, causing the credulous ringsider to flee into the crowd. The riled animal gave chase, forcing audience members to leap over chairs as they dispersed. After a few moments, the bear was caught by his trainer and led back into the squared circle to begin the contest.

Both combatants then stood in the centre of the ring to receive instructions from the referee, although it's not clear to what extent the bear understood them. Dunlop made a show of remonstrating with the referee about his fear of Terrible Ted biting or clawing him - both of which were unlikely to happen, given that the bear was muzzled and had his claws cut short. After the trainer reassured Dunlop that grappling with the bear was quite safe, the two contestants tangled with one another as Ted stood on his hind legs and wrapped his arms around his opponent, before Dunlop responded with a neck vice. Ted escaped the hold by shaking his head and then chased Dunlop around the ring. The novelty of the pursuit soon wore off though and Ted took a seat in the middle of the ring and yawned extravagantly.

In a bid to continue the spectacle, Dunlop reached over and prodded Ted, who then swatted his adversary's rear - which Dunlop sold by rolling around on the mat in mock agony. After Dunlop stood back up, he repeated his previous tactic of kicking the animal. Ted, apparently infuriated, charged after Dunlop, who vaulted over the ropes to escape the ring and absconded down the aisle towards the changing rooms. The bear gave chase, again scattering the crowd, while the referee declared that the match was a no-contest as both wrestlers had left the ring.

As attitudes to animal welfare changed, the era of the wrestling bear came to an end in the early 1980s. One bear, named Victor, had his licence to wrestle revoked by the Virginia Athletic Commission in October 1981 because 'he has too much facial hair and is mentally incompetent.'

OVERZEALOUS FANS

FIRE
FIRE
IMPROMPTU FINISH
EXPLOSION
INJURY
SURREAL

CHAPTER 8:

ABSURD IDEAS

The Sheik & Sabu vs Atsushi Onita & Tarzan Goto

Sanda, Japan, May 1992

Violent gimmick match called off in under two minutes after ring goes up in flames

It seemed like the perfect idea. Pioneering Japanese promotion FMW focused on impossibly violent gimmick matches that often involved the use of explosives. But explosive charges don't come cheap and, as a low-budget indie concern, the company was always trying to cut costs. So it came up with a concept that it thought provided the same gruesome spectacle at a fraction of the cost: a match in which the ring was surrounded by fire.

For this tag contest, the ropes were taken down and replaced by barbed wire, around which were wrapped a dozen thick wads of fabric soaked in paraffin. The Japanese team of Atsushi Onita and Tarzan Goto entered the ring first, closely followed by their American opponents The Sheik (a Michigan native but billed as being from Syria) and his nephew Sabu. The Sheik was 65 at the time and, beyond playing up to his maniacal persona, was limited in what he could do physically – he looked to be in pain just walking to the ring. He'd be in even more pain on leaving it.

The scrap began with Onita clobbering The Sheik, while Goto and Sabu took it in turns to pummel one another. Meanwhile, stagehands began to light the fabric around the ring. Within seconds, it was apparent that the flames were far too large: an excess of flammable material had been used and a strong breeze (the show was held in an outdoor arena) helped to fan the blaze. Far from providing the illusion of violence, the match placed all four wrestlers and the referee in genuine peril. Nonetheless, the grapplers briefly continued with their pre-planned exchanges – The Sheik even stabbed Onita in the forehead with a fork, his weapon of choice.

But it soon became difficult to see what was taking place as the flames were so high the participants were obscured. The wind blew the fire on to the edge of the mat, which ignited due to the paraffin dripping on to it from the rags above. The referee grimaced in the heat and, less than two minutes in, called off the match and ordered the wrestlers to leave the ring.

Sabu dove under the bottom strand of barbed wire to escape the inferno. The other wrestlers crawled out of the opposite side of the ring to the relative safety of the floor, while attendants hopelessly flung buckets of water at the flames, to little effect. Onita and The Sheik briefly continued the performance with a tussle at ringside, which culminated in The Sheik throwing a fireball at his opponent using magician's flash paper.

Even though it was Onita who was left laying as he sold the effects of the fireball, it was The Sheik who was legitimately injured during the debacle: he failed to duck far enough beneath the flames on exiting the ring and was hospitalised with horrific burns to his back. The event ended with the venue filled with smoke, the ring reduced to a burnt-out husk, as a small fire smouldered at ringside. FMW stuck to the explosives after that.

Al Snow vs Big Boss Man

Charlotte, North Carolina, September 1999

Grudge match descends into farce as dogs empty bowels at ringside

Any feud that is centred around someone inadvertently eating their own dog is never going to end well. Yet this was the basis of the 1999 grudge between Al Snow and the Big Boss Man – a premise that was, incredibly, inspired by genuine events. 'They based the angle on a real-life situation where [wrestling manager] Mr Fuji had a neighbour with a dog,' says Snow. 'The dog kept barking and, one day, Fuji killed it while the neighbour was gone, and then invited him over for dinner and fed it to him.'

After the Boss Man perpetrated a similarly heinous act involving Snow's pet pooch, the dispute culminated with a gimmick match – dubbed the 'kennel from hell' – at an event called *Unforgiven*. It was the first time the WWF had ever promoted such a contest. Tellingly, it would also be the last. On paper, the concept was an intriguing one: the ring would be surrounded by a cage, which itself would be encased in a second, larger cage lowered from the ceiling. The space between the two structures would be filled with a pack of bloodthirsty fighting dogs, giving the appearance that the two wrestlers were putting themselves in genuine peril. In practice, the match was a disaster of unprecedented proportions.

'The idea was that the dogs would circle between the cages like sharks,' explains Snow. 'I had insisted from the very beginning that they had to get properly trained attack animals that would act on command.' Instead, the WWF only made arrangements to procure the canines on the morning of the show, which they did by phoning a veterinary clinic and obtaining a list of local Rottweiler owners. 'Every dog had a different owner,' says Snow. 'I asked them what training the dogs had: one had some obedience training and that was it. It was absurd.'

The result was that, far from the ring being patrolled by a pack of killer hounds baying for blood, the animals couldn't have been less interested in the feuding grapplers. They instead spent the entire match emptying their bladders and bowels around the ringside area and humping one another.

'The entire gimmick of the match was based solely upon the animals, who were out there urinating, defecating and fornicating to the point where they couldn't show them on camera, let alone use them in a manner that would put somebody in jeopardy,' sighs Snow. 'In the end, the biggest spot involving the dogs was when one of the owners, who looked as if he weighed 350lbs, tripped over and big-splashed his own dog on the way out of the ring.'

After some painfully lacklustre action inside the squared circle, Snow brought an end to the fiasco when he clobbered the Boss Man with a mannequin's head and then escaped the twin cages, while the supposedly ferocious mutts took no notice of him whatsoever. 'Basically, we were handed – in every sense – a big pile of dog shit,' he says. 'It was embarrassing, it really was.'

Fabulous Freebirds vs Doom

Montgomery, Alabama, February 1991

Time-travelling tag champs lose titles before they win them

Today, wrestling fans expect to watch shows that are either broadcast live (*WWE Raw*) or shown on television just a few days after they are taped at arenas (*WWE Smackdown*, *TNA Impact*). But prior to wrestling's explosion on cable TV in the US, which was heralded by the debuts of *Raw* in January 1993 and *WCW Monday Nitro* in September 1995, promoters relied on weekly syndicated programmes, which were shown on local affiliate stations around the country.

Whereas modern wrestling shows generally take place on a rolling weekly basis, when syndicated programming ruled the airwaves, matches were filmed weeks in advance at mammoth tapings that covered up to a month's worth of telly in one go. Naturally, this led to some bizarre continuity errors between what live audiences saw and where the episodic TV storylines had reached at the time, not least when it came to title changes.

The WWF and WCW would get around this, somewhat, by only acknowledging that a belt had changed hands once the title bout had aired on television, even if it had actually taken place at a TV taping days or even weeks earlier. While this would often mean that champions would defend titles at house shows (non-televised events) that they had already lost, such madness was taken to its illogical conclusion by WCW in 1991 when the Fabulous Freebirds' second WCW world tag team title reign ended before it started.

The Freebirds duo of Jimmy Garvin and Michael Hayes won the tag belts from Doom (Ron Simmons and Butch Reed) at the *WrestleWar* pay-per-view, which took place in Phoenix, Arizona on 24 February. But they had already *lost* the titles to brothers Rick and Scott Steiner at a TV taping in Montgomery, Alabama six days earlier. The title loss wasn't broadcast until 9 March so, to viewers at home, everything was in chronological order and the Freebirds 'officially' held the straps for 13 days.

DOOMED CONCEPT

EXPLOSION

Vampiro vs 6-Pac

Los Angeles, California, November 2006

MTV title match culminates with wrestlers plummeting into exploding coffin

MTV's vision of pro wrestling was as absurdly over-the-top as it was short-lived. **Wrestling Society X**, as the show was called, was based around ultra-brief bouts that were laden with aerial manoeuvres and gimmickry - one match even included a spot in which a wrestler 'electrocuted' his opponent with a loose electrical cable.

This match between Vampiro (billed as 'from the darkest depths of hell') and former WWF star Sean '6-Pac' Waltman, to determine the first ever WSX champion, was typical of the fare on offer. The two raced through a match, with none of the psychology or attempts at story-telling usually associated with pro wresting exhibitions.

Waltman performed a somersault dive out of the ring, while Vampiro retaliated by flinging him groin-first into a post. Vampiro followed this with another low blow and a tombstone piledriver off the ring apron on to a coffin that had been wheeled to ringside at the start of the match. The two combatants crashed through the wooden lid into the casket, at which point a series of explosives placed under the coffin were detonated, sending sparks and smoke billowing into the air.

The referee counted to three and handed the WSX title to Vampiro as he clambered out of the ruined coffin, spitting stage blood. The audience reacted with suitably histrionic whoops and cheers - not so much because they were absorbed by the action but more because they were actually TV extras employed to play the role of ringside fans. The entire incident was so hammy you could have made a sandwich out of it. Indeed, viewers were determinedly underwhelmed by the (even by wrestling standards) incredibly contrived-looking tussles: the US ratings were so poor that the series was pulled and its final episode never aired.

David Arquette & Dallas Page vs Eric Bischoff & Jeff Jarrett

Syracuse, New York, April 2000

DOOMED CONCEPT

Scream actor wins world title... from his own tag team partner

When actor David Arquette debuted on WCW television in April 2000, seasoned viewers knew it was going to conclude badly. They just didn't know how badly. Arquette, best known for his role in the *Scream* franchise, had recently starred in the critically-panned wrestling movie *Ready to Rumble*. It was all the excuse WCW needed to crowbar Arquette into a storyline of its own.

Jeff Jarrett had just lost the WCW world championship - the highest accolade that any grappler in the company could achieve - to his rival 'Diamond' Dallas Page in a cage match. An entire episode of TV show *WCW Thunder* was then constructed around Jarrett blaming Arquette for his title loss, even though Arquette had nothing to do with it - the sort of gaping chasm in a narrative arc for which WCW booker Vince Russo was notorious. The show then culminated in a tag team match that pitted Page and Arquette against Jarrett and WCW boss Eric Bischoff. In a stipulation that defied any rational explanation, whoever garnered the pinfall would become the new WCW champion.

Page soon attempted to pin Jarrett but was thwarted by special referee Kimberly Page - his real-life wife but storyline ex-wife. Kimberley stopped counting after one as she broke a nail, preventing Page from retaining his title. Meanwhile, non-wrestlers Bischoff and Arquette brawled around the ringside area and up the aisle with surprising ferocity, before disappearing backstage.

Arquette eventually staggered back to the ring, shortly before Kimberly was 'knocked unconscious' by being kissed by DDP. Jarrett then thwacked Page with the title belt, while Arquette tackled Bischoff to the mat. With the special ref out of commission, a second referee pelted down to the ring, completely ignored the fact that Jarrett was covering Page and instead counted the pinfall as Bischoff was covered by Arquette, leaving the actor as world champion - even though former champion Page (who had only won the title the day before) was his tag partner and, in conjunction with Arquette, had actually won the match. Equally absurd was the fact that DDP was in no way upset at having just lost the promotion's richest prize, a title previously held by such notable wrestling stars as Ric Flair, Hulk Hogan, Bret Hart and Randy Savage.

Arquette had been a wrestling fan since childhood and was well aware of the extent to which his title reign would devalue the championship. As such, he petitioned *not* to win the belt - but Russo was convinced that the publicity garnered by the stunt would outweigh the objections of existing WCW fans. Arquette lost the title to Jarrett after only 12 days as the result of a triple-decker cage match, in which he double-crossed his 'friend' DDP and clubbed him over the head with a guitar. Arquette's entire wrestling career lasted for less than a month. He did, however, make one final appearance on a wrestling TV show: during a February 2002 episode of *WWF Smackdown*, he was dressed as if he was destitute and was seen holding a sign that read, 'Former world champion.'

The Bushwhackers & Men on a Mission vs The Headshrinkers, Bam Bam Bigelow & Bastion Booger

Boston, Massachusetts, November 1993

Catastrophically bad match goes to prove that clowns really are evil

Back in 1993, the WWF was in the midst of both a commercial and creative slump. In contrast to the more human characters of the 'Attitude' era that followed five years later, there was a focus on cartoony grapplers aimed at young children. Hence Doink the Clown – a bottom-of-the-bill attraction who was portrayed by a number of journeymen performers and confirmation, if any were needed, that the WWF really was a circus.

The sheer stupidity of the concept reached its nadir at the 1993 *Survivor Series*, when an entire four-man squad was composed of established wrestlers – tag teams The Bushwhackers and Men on a Mission – who were clad in Doink's trademark greasepaint and green wig combo. Cue 11 minutes of 'hilarious' japes that began with one of the clowns riding around ringside on a child's scooter. The idiocy continued as Luke Williams of The Bushwhackers bit Bastion Booger – a fat man dressed in a gimp outfit – on the arse. Headshrinker Samu was eliminated after he sunk his teeth into what he thought was a balloon but was, in fact, a water bomb.

His tag partner Fatu slipped over on a banana skin… but only after he'd thrown it into the centre of the ring as it wasn't in the correct position for the stunt. Team Doink won the debacle after Men on a Mission's Mabel – a 6ft 6in-tall man clad in purple and gold dungarees – splashed Bam Bam Bigelow, before all four clowns piled on to him to secure the pinfall.

Latin American Xchange vs Beer Money, Inc

OVERZEALOUS FANS

Houston, Texas, July 2008

Loony stipulation allows fans to whip hated tag team with leather straps

Lumberjack matches are among the least spectacular gimmick bouts ever conceived. The ring is surrounded by wrestlers and, if anyone involved in the match is thrown out of it, the 'lumberjacks' will throw a few punches at them and then roll them back through the ropes.

On rare occasions though, such matches are given a spectacularly barmy twist when the role of the lumberjacks is played by fans, as was the case for this contest between the Latin American Xchange (Homicide and Hernandez) and Beer Money, Inc (Robert Roode and James Storm) at TNA pay-per-view *Victory Road.*

What the promotion billed as '12 angry fans' (actually competition winners) were equipped with leather straps and encouraged to whip Roode and Storm whenever they left the six-sided ring. In previous contests with such stipulations - notably a 1991 meeting between Terry Funk and Jerry Lawler - the fans were so afraid of the wrestlers that they were reluctant to become physically involved with proceedings.

But that was far from the case here. As soon as Roode was flung outside the ring by Homicide, four strap-wielding fans rounded on him and whipped him as hard as they could. When Storm subsequently ran around the ringside area, every lumberjack attacked him as he scurried past: in selling the blows, Storm looked as if he was walking barefoot across a hot patio.

The audience-inflicted thrashings continued whenever either member of Beer Money ventured through the ropes: at one point, Roode took refuge under the ring and, by the end of the confrontation, Storm's back was covered with angry-looking welts. LAX, unsurprisingly, went on to win the match and retain their TNA tag titles.

Ultimate Warrior vs Bobby Heenan

New York, June 1988

Chubby wrestling manager forced to dress as weasel after loss to face-painted muscle man

Bobby 'The Brain' Heenan was never afraid to make himself look stupid. As the WWF's leading manager of the 1980s, suffering indignities was his stock in trade – even if it meant having to dress up in a weasel costume. The weasel suit match was a bizarre speciality bout peculiar to Heenan: whoever won such a contest (something that Heenan never did) was then permitted to place his unfortunate opponent in what appeared to be an outsize Babygro, replete with paws and a tail.

Heenan first used the gimmick in bouts against Greg Gagne in the AWA in 1980. But the weasel suit match secured its highest profile during a run of WWF bouts between 'The Brain' and future WWF champion Jim 'Ultimate Warrior' Hellwig in summer 1988. The visual of a pudgy middle-aged bloke in a singlet confronting a 6ft 2in face-painted maniac pumped to the gills with steroids was as comical as it was preposterous.

The slapstick matches – including one at Madison Square Garden – followed a strict template. Heenan entered the ring with a look of grave concern on his face. He was soon followed by the Warrior, a hopeless worker whose best move involved shaking the top rope violently, while headbanging to a tune that only he could hear. Warrior came to the ring holding the weasel suit and it wasn't difficult to figure out who would be wearing it in a few minutes' time.

Warrior draped the suit in the corner of the ring and then stood on the second rope to play to the crowd. Heenan raced up behind the long-haired bodybuilder and unleashed a series of forearm blows that had no effect whatsoever. Hellwig pounded his own chest, as 'The Brain' jumped outside the ring to evade his opponent. The farce continued with Warrior chasing Heenan around the ringside area, before he finally caught him by hiding behind the ring apron.

Just as it appeared as if the match was over, the wily manager jabbed Warrior in the throat with a foreign object, causing the muscle man to act as if he was unable to breathe. Heenan repeated the tactic, in between hiding the weapon from the referee in his tights. But when Heenan threw Warrior into the ropes, Warrior grabbed the object and retaliated with a series of chops to the chest, causing his foe to take an exaggerated fall to the mat. Warrior followed up by sending Heenan into the turnbuckles, where he took further exaggerated nose dives to the canvas. The massacre ended when Warrior placed Heenan in a sleeper hold: 'The Brain' quickly feigned unconsciousness.

The referee called for the bell, which was the signal for Warrior to squeeze the inert manager into the furry outfit, before he woke Heenan up by slapping him in the face. Heenan gradually came to and, on realising that he was clad in the costume, started chasing his own tail while desperately trying to extract himself from the suit. Inevitably, he plummeted to the mat, where he continued his frantic bid to escape from the fancy dress garb. When he was finally out of the costume, he flung it in the air in disgust. With perfect comic timing, he made sure that it landed on his head.

Don Muraco vs Rudy Diamond

Allentown, Pennsylvania, August 1983

Intercontinental champion interrupts match to feast on meatball sandwich

WWF television matches during the 1980s followed a predictable formula. A prominent grappler would face an unknown hopeful, who was instructed to provide little if any offence and would be soundly beaten within a matter of minutes. Such 'squash matches' provided no drama regarding who would win, as the star wrestler was never placed in any jeopardy. During one such contest against perennial loser Rudy Diamond, Intercontinental champion Don Muraco decided that he might as well take the opportunity to combine his match with the consumption of a light snack.

His manager, Captain Lou Albano, came to ringside clutching a meatball sandwich and a large cup of Coke. In between comprehensively destroying his doomed opponent, Muraco would wander over to Albano in order to have a bite of sandwich and a refreshing slurp of soft drink. The bout culminated with Muraco setting up Diamond for his piledriver finisher. But instead of completing the manoeuvre, he again mooched over to the corner for another mouthful of sandwich - this time fed to him by the Captain - while still holding on to Diamond. Suitably fed, Muraco ambled back into the centre of the ring and concluded the move by driving Diamond's head into the mat - after which he scored the pinfall, while still chewing.

But the fun wasn't over. On exiting the ring after the match, Albano tripped over and plummeted to the floor. Muraco howled with laughter as a TV camera zoomed in to reveal that his manager had, in fact, slipped over on a meatball that had dropped on to the ring steps. Later the same night, Muraco won a second squash match against Rocco Verona, although he chose not to combine the contest with another nosh. Perhaps he had indigestion.

Comedy

Shane Douglas vs Billy Kidman

Cincinnati, Ohio, July 2000

Grappler goes home with three women after 'accidentally' swallowing Viagra pills during match

COCK UP

SURREAL

Towards the end of its existence, WCW presented some of the most bizarre concepts ever seen in a major wrestling promotion - not least a match fought under 'Viagra on a pole' rules on an episode of *Monday Nitro*. The bout's execution was as flawed as its concept.

A large bottled marked 'Viagra' was hung from a pole placed in the corner of the ring and announcer Tony Schiavone explained that if you grabbed the bottle, you were allowed to use it as a weapon. During the first few minutes of action, the trio of announcers did little to hide their disdain for the ludicrous showdown.

After Douglas drove Kidman to the mat with his Pittsburgh Plunge finisher, he climbed the corner of the ring in an attempt to reach the bottle but he was powerbombed by Kidman. 'Now, Kidman, he's going up for the bottle of Viagra,' said Schiavone. Unable to hide the melancholy in his voice, he added, 'I never thought I'd say that in a wrestling match.'

Kidman hit Douglas with an inverted facebuster, which bought him enough time to clamber up the pole and grab the bottle of pills. But Douglas struck back with a suplex, after which he was supposed to retrieve the bottle from Kidman and smash it over his head, with the 'hilarious' result that some of the tablets accidentally fell into Kidman's mouth.

The bottle had already been inadvertently broken though when Kidman landed from the suplex. Douglas picked up its remains and, for reasons that were never made clear (even the announcers couldn't make sense of it), was declared the winner by the ref. Kidman, meanwhile, was forced to improvise and, off-camera, picked up some of the pills that had dropped on to the mat and stuffed them into his mouth in a bid to insinuate that they had somehow fallen in his gob by mistake. The clearly excited Kidman was later shown leaving the building with three members of the Nitro Girls dance troupe.

Mike Samples, Mad Man Pondo, Bad Boy Hido & 2 Tuff Tony vs Abdullah Kobayashi, Daikokubo Benkei, Men's Teioh & Ryuji Ito

Tokyo, Japan, August 2003

Bonkers wrestling show takes place inside replica house constructed in arena

Big Japan Pro Wrestling's August 2003 show in Tokyo's Korakuen Hall tore the house down – literally. In lieu of matches taking place in a ring, the audience faced an elaborate stage set that replicated a fully-furnished two-storey dwelling, with every bout taking place in the plywood building-within-a-building (supposedly the home of company president Shinya Kojika). You couldn't fault the attention to detail: the fridge was stocked with food and drink, the 'front garden' was filled with plants, there was clothing in the wardrobes and even photos on the living room walls. For added authenticity, many of the items were from Kojika's actual home.

The event was sponsored by an adult entertainment company, which meant that the abode was constructed by a team that usually built sets for porn films. 'It was almost 100 per cent a real house,' says Mike Samples, one of the wrestlers on the show. 'A little more work and someone could have lived in it.'

The opening contests included a 'scramble bunkhouse kitchen deathmatch', in which Mad Man Pondo defeated Abdullah Kobayashi after tipping a bowl of raw eggs over his head and diving on to him from the kitchen sink, and a 'toilet chain deathmatch'. For that particular clash between Samples and Daikokubo Benkei, the entire match was fought in the downstairs lavatory and ended after Samples stuck a toilet plunger over Benkei's face and then forced him to submit by flushing his head down the loo. 'I have never been a fan of comedy in wrestling,' says Samples. 'But Benkei didn't have a problem with it, so neither did I.'

Following a tag team match in which a vacuum cleaner, a telephone and a stuffed deer's head were used as weapons, the presentation climaxed with an eight-man bout featuring every grappler who had appeared on the undercard, during which the faux house was completely trashed. 'The idea was to tear it down as much as we possibly could because it had to be gone so quickly,' admits Samples. 'It had to be out of the venue by midnight or they had to pay another day's rent. Precision teamwork at its best!'

To wit, it was not so much a wrestling match as much as a demolition derby. The early part of the scrap was highlighted by Men's Teioh attacking 2 Tuff Tony with a samurai sword before backdropping him through a patio door. Other objects utilised as impromptu weaponry included a bicycle, an acoustic guitar, a micro scooter and a tiger skin rug. ('We were careful not to destroy Kojika's personal items,' says Samples.) After only a few minutes, the house was littered with debris and broken furniture; the front row of the audience hid behind umbrellas to protect themselves from the fallout.

Just to ensure that the building was completely wrecked, another troupe of wrestlers wearing hard hats charged into the hall in the middle of the brawl. Armed with sledgehammers, they began knocking down what remained of the house – even the garden wall got a good kicking. The bedlam was finally brought to an end when Ryuji Ito wrapped himself in a vest made from barbed wire and leapt from the house on to Samples' tag partner 2 Tuff Tony to score the three-count. 'It was just another day in Japan for me,' says Samples.

Road Warriors vs Midnight Express

Atlanta, Georgia, November 198

Unfortunate manager blows out knee after ill-advised tumble from scaffolding

The scaffold match is one of the barmiest wrestling gimmicks ever conceived. It was invented by wrestler/promoter Jerry Jarrett in 1971 but its use was largely confined to the Tennessee area until the 1980s. A pair of scaffold towers are constructed on either side of the ring. Between them, they support a narrow walkway above the squared circle. For this match between the Road Warriors (Michael 'Hawk' Hegstrand and Joe 'Animal' Laurinaitis) and the Midnight Express ('Beautiful' Bobby Eaton and Dennis Condrey, who was later replaced by Stan Lane), the platform was placed at a height of 21ft above the ring. To win the bout, a team had to throw its opponents off the gangplank into the ring below.

DOOMED CONCEPT

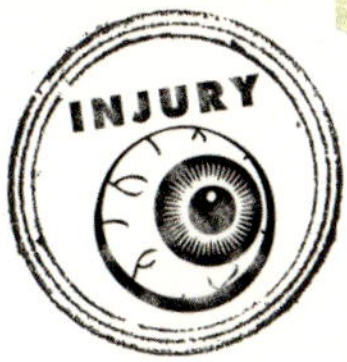

The lack of room and chance of serious injury meant that the match contained no grappling at all, as it posed the risk of someone accidentally falling off the structure, a problem compounded by the fact that Hawk had broken his ankle while wrestling in Japan. Instead, the duelling duos spent most of the contest clinging to the rickety steel platform and exchanging punches. The heel Midnight Express attempted to gain the advantage by throwing powder into the eyes of their face-painted, prodigiously muscular adversaries (Hawk admitted to injecting rhesus monkey hormones in a bid to improve his physique and was taking such large doses of steroids in the 1980s that he woke up each morning wanting to kill someone).

The *Mad Max*-inspired Warriors soon regained the advantage with a barrage of blows. The contest ended with all four grapplers dangling off the underside of the platform. Condrey plummeted to the ring first (he later said that he felt as if he'd been hit by a car), closely followed by Eaton, who landed awkwardly on one leg and sprained his ankle.

But the highlight was scripted to take place *after* the Roadies had won. At the behest of booker Dusty Rhodes, Hawk chased Express manager Jim Cornette around the ringside area. Cornette then made the tactical error of trying to escape by clambering up the scaffold, where he was met by Animal. With nowhere else to go, the hapless manager crawled off the side of the platform and grabbed hold of the bottom of it, a position from which he swung wildly for a few seconds.

Inevitably, he dropped into the ring, where he was supposed to be caught by his on-screen bodyguard Big Bubba Rogers (later Big Boss Man in the WWF). But he fell so quickly that Rogers had no chance to break his fall and he instead plunged straight to the mat. On landing, Cornette's right leg bent sideways and his head smacked against Bubba's knee, momentarily knocking him out. With Rogers' help, he then managed to hobble backstage. Cornette was unable to walk the next day and subsequently underwent surgery for a torn anterior cruciate ligament and severe cartilage damage. He now only has a third of the cartilage in his right knee.

Gerald Brisco vs Pat Patterson

DOOMED CONCEPT

SURREAL

Boston, Massachusetts, June 2000

Old-school stars destroy legacy with wince-inducing drag act

In their 1970s heydays, both Gerald Brisco (a former NWA world tag team champion) and Pat Patterson (the first holder of the WWF Intercontinental title) were highly respected performers. But they managed to comprehensively overshadow any previous accomplishments in June 2000 thanks to a single, horribly misjudged match.

An entirely implausible storyline involving the two old-timers culminated in a contest for the hardcore title at *King of the Ring*, which was contested under 'evening gown' rules: both men fought while dressed as women and the match could only be won by stripping your opponent down to his undergarments.

Brisco had donned lipstick, a floor-length black frock and high-heeled boots for the occasion. The 59-year-old Patterson, meanwhile, entered the ring clad in a platinum blond fright wig and a fetching red sequined gown. The former Intercontinental champ took the early lead when he kneed Brisco in the balls, stuffed a banana in his mouth and rubbed a sanitary towel in his face that he had retrieved from his pants. When Brisco struck back with a low blow of his own, commentator Jim Ross could only say, 'This is hideous.'

After just two minutes of the farce, wrestler Crash Holly pelted down to the ring, twatted Patterson over the head with a dustbin and pinned him to win the hardcore belt – which any grappler was able to challenge for at any time. Brisco and Patterson were left writhing in the ring in women's underwear. Even by the WWF's low-rent standards, it was one of the most pointless spectacles ever conceived.

Team 3D vs Curry Man & Shark Boy

Norfolk, Virginia, March 2008

Comedy

Fishing rod, net and fresh catch used as surreal weapons in 'fish market street fight'

As tag teams go, it's certainly one of the odder ones: Shark Boy, replete with mask that has a stitched-on fin, and Curry Man ('He's hot, he's spicy, he tastes great!'), clad in headwear that's topped with a bowl of curry. To add to the wacky outfits, when they faced Team 3D (formerly the Dudley Boyz) at TNA's *Destination X* pay-per-view event, it was contested under 'fish market street fight' rules, in which stands packed with wet fish were set up in the aisle.

Curry Man (actually respected grappler Christopher Daniels) brought a fishing rod into the ring, attached a chocolate cake to the end of it and dangled it over the ropes. Team 3D's Brother Ray was unable to resist the sugary treat and attempted to scoff it – with the result that he was 'hooked' on the end of the line, enabling Curry Man to reel him into the squared circle. Ray made a comeback by backdropping Curry Man into a tray of seafood, before flinging fish into the unfortunate audience – one woman was hit right in the face – which responded by throwing the creatures back at the wrestlers.

Ray took a bite out of a raw fish (a shock tactic previously employed by WWF tag champions the Wild Samoans in the early 1980s), while Team 3D cohort Johnny Devine trapped Curry Man in a net, which also housed a large crab. Brother Ray then twonked the hapless Curry Man in the groin with a sea bass – but only after French kissing the fish first. The suitably preposterous finish came when Devine accidentally threw powder into Brother Ray's eyes, who then inadvertently performed his finishing move on his own partner, Brother Devon, allowing him to be pinned by Shark Boy.

ANIMAL

Jake Roberts vs Rick Martel

Los Angeles, California,
March 1991

Grapplers end feud with match at biggest show of year... while blindfolded

Even for an industry built on the audience's suspension of disbelief being taken to its very limits, the blindfold match is a daft concept. This rarely-used gimmick (which dates back to the 1930s) requires the participants to each wear a black hood that covers their entire head and, supposedly, leaves them in complete darkness.

The WWF deemed that such a contest would be the ideal culmination to a feud between Rick 'The Model' Martel and Jake 'The Snake' Roberts. As part of his 'model' shtick, Martel repeated the ploy first used by Gorgeous George and carried an atomiser, with which he would spray the ring and his opponents in order to make them fresh enough for his sensitive nose. During an episode of interview segment *The Brother Love Show* taped in September 1990, Martel sprayed Roberts in the eyes with the cologne, which - according to the storyline - temporarily blinded Roberts, who wore white contact lenses for months to mimic the damage to his corneas.

Jake's blindfold revenge match took place at *WrestleMania VII* at the Los Angeles Sports Arena. He had, by now, regained his sight but the idea was that, having previously experienced impaired vision, he would have the advantage over his dastardly opponent. Of course, both wrestlers were able to see through the hoods but had to pretend otherwise. As such, they spent most of the encounter stumbling around the ring 'unable' to find one another.

Once the bell rang, Martel feigned panic, while Roberts coolly used the crowd's cheers in a bid to direct himself towards his opponent. Roberts finally managed to grab Martel's leg, before 'The Model' stumbled backwards and fell to the mat. Martel recovered and threw his crafty adversary into the ropes, only for 'The Snake' to avoid Martel's backdrop attempt by simply running in a different direction. Martel suffered further humiliation when he elbow-dropped the empty canvas, mistakenly thinking that Roberts was lying beneath him. Inevitably, Martel then attempted to attack the referee, believing that he'd finally located his foe. The nonsense was eventually wrapped up when Roberts escaped from Martel's Boston crab finisher and 'knocked him out' by forcing his head into the mat with a DDT. For the coup de grâce, Roberts retrieved an enormous Burmese python from a sack that he had earlier placed in the corner of the ring and wrapped the snake around 'The Model' – probably the most entertaining moment of the entire charade.

The routine was reprised on occasion, with equally lacklustre results. Triple H defeated D'Lo Brown in such a match on an episode of *Raw* in October 2002, a bout that was highlighted by Helmsley talking trash into an empty space, erroneously thinking that Brown was in front of him. Five years later, rival promotion TNA revived the gimmick with a blindfold cage fight between former tag partners Chris Harris and James Storm. The shambolic brawl was one of the worst matches of the decade – not least because the combatants' hoods kept falling off, meaning that even the most determinedly naive viewer was unable to buy into the cartoon daftness.

El Gigante, Sting, Rick Steiner & Scott Steiner vs Big Van Vader, Diamond Studd, Cactus Jack & Abdullah the Butcher

Chattanooga, Tennessee, October 1991

Ludicrous caged showdown ends with wrestler strapped to 'electric chair'

WCW came up with some real stinkers in its time but one of the best – well, worst – of them all was the Chamber of Horrors match from 1991's *Halloween Havoc*. The four-on-four scrap took place in a large cage and the only way to win was to place a member of the opposing team in a 'chair of torture' – which was lowered into the ring a few minutes into the bout – and then pulling the 'fatal lever' attached to the side of the enclosure.

The only thing that died though was the audience's interest, especially when a close-up camera shot halfway through the bout made it clear that the switch was already in the 'on' position. As if the whole concept wasn't daft enough to begin with, once the chair was in the ring, it took up so much space that it was impossible for the participants to execute any moves other than rudimentary kicks, punches or weapon shots.

In addition, referee Nick Patrick was fitted with a camera, giving viewers a ref's-eye view of proceedings. It was, to be fair, a load of camp old nonsense. After 12 minutes of non-action, Rick Steiner finally forced Abdullah the Butcher – an entirely bald, grossly obese man with scars in his head so deep he could balance coins in them – into the chair. Teammate Mick 'Cactus Jack' Foley then accidentally threw the lever, thinking that it was Steiner who was in the hot seat, and fried poor old Abdullah.

Abdullah survived the mock execution and went on to open a restaurant in Atlanta called Abdullah the Butcher's House of Ribs and Chinese Food. According to one review, the service is 'prompt and friendly'.

Bibliography

Shaun Assael and Mike Mooneyham, *Sex, Lies and Headlocks: The Real Story of Vince McMahon and the World Wrestling Federation*, Crown Publishers, 2002

Steve Austin with Jim Ross, *The Stone Cold Truth*, Pocket Books, 2003

Tom Billington with Alison Coleman, *Pure Dynamite*, SW Publishing, 1999

Freddie Blassie with Keith Elliot Greenberg, *Listen, You Pencil Neck Geeks*, Pocket Books, 2004

Bob Calhoun, *Beer, Blood & Cornmeal: Seven Years of Incredibly Strange Wrestling*, ECW Press, 2008

John Capouya, *Gorgeous George: The Outrageous Bad-Boy Wrestler Who Created American Pop Culture*, Harper Entertainment, 2008

Jim Cornette with Tim Ash, *The Midnight Express and Jim Cornette: 25th Anniversary Scrapbook*, self-published, 2009

Lillian Ellison with Larry Platt, *The Fabulous Moolah: First Goddess of the Squared Circle*, Regan Books, 2002

Ric Flair with Keith Elliot Greenberg, *To Be the Man*, Pocket Books, 2004

Mick Foley, *Have a Nice Day! A Tale of Blood and Sweatsocks*, Regan Books, 1999

Terry Funk with Scott E Williams, *Terry Funk: More Than Just Hardcore*, Sports Publishing LLC, 2005

Simon Garfield, *The Wrestling*, Faber and Faber, 1996

Bret Hart, *Hitman: My Real Life in the Cartoon World of Wrestling*, Random House Canada, 2007

Thomas Hauser, *Muhammad Ali: His Life and Times*, Robson Books, 1991

Bobby Heenan with Steve Anderson, *Bobby the Brain: Wrestling's Bad Boy Tells All*, Triumph Books, 2002

Tim Hornbaker, *National Wrestling Alliance: The Untold Story of the Monopoly That Strangled Pro Wrestling*, ECW Press, 2007

Fred Hornby et al, *The History of Professional Wrestling #3: Madison Square Garden 1880-1999*, Crowbar Press, 2000

Michael Krugman, *Andre the Giant: A Legendary Life*, Pocket Books, 2009

Jerry Lawler with Doug Asheville, *It's Good to be the King... Sometimes*, Pocket Books, 2003

John Lister, *Turning the Tables: The Story of Extreme Championship Wrestling*, Exposure Publishing, 2005

Thom Loverro, *The Rise & Fall of ECW*, Pocket Books, 2006

Findlay Martin (editor), *Power Slam* magazine, SW Publishing

Larry Matysik and Barbara Goodish, *Brody: The Triumph and Tragedy of Wrestling's Rebel*, ECW Press, 2007

Dave Meltzer, *Tributes*, Powerbomb, 1998

Dave Meltzer (editor), *Wrestling Observer Newsletter*, self-published

Greg Oliver and Steven Johnson, *The Pro Wrestling Hall of Fame: The Heels*, ECW Press, 2007

Mike Quackenbush and Slade Bracey, *Chikara Yearbook: 2009 Edition*, Instant Publisher, 2009

Harley Race with Gerry Tritz, *King of the Ring: The Harley Race Story*, Sports Publishing LLC, 2004

RD Reynolds and Bryan Alvarez, *The Death of WCW*, ECW Press, 2004

Bruno Sammartino with Bob Michelucci and Paul McCollough, *Bruno Sammartino: An Autobiography of Wrestling's Living Legend*, Imagine, 1990

Lou Thesz with Kit Bauman, *Hooker: An Authentic Wrestler's Adventures Inside the Bizarre World of Pro Wrestling*, self-published, 1995

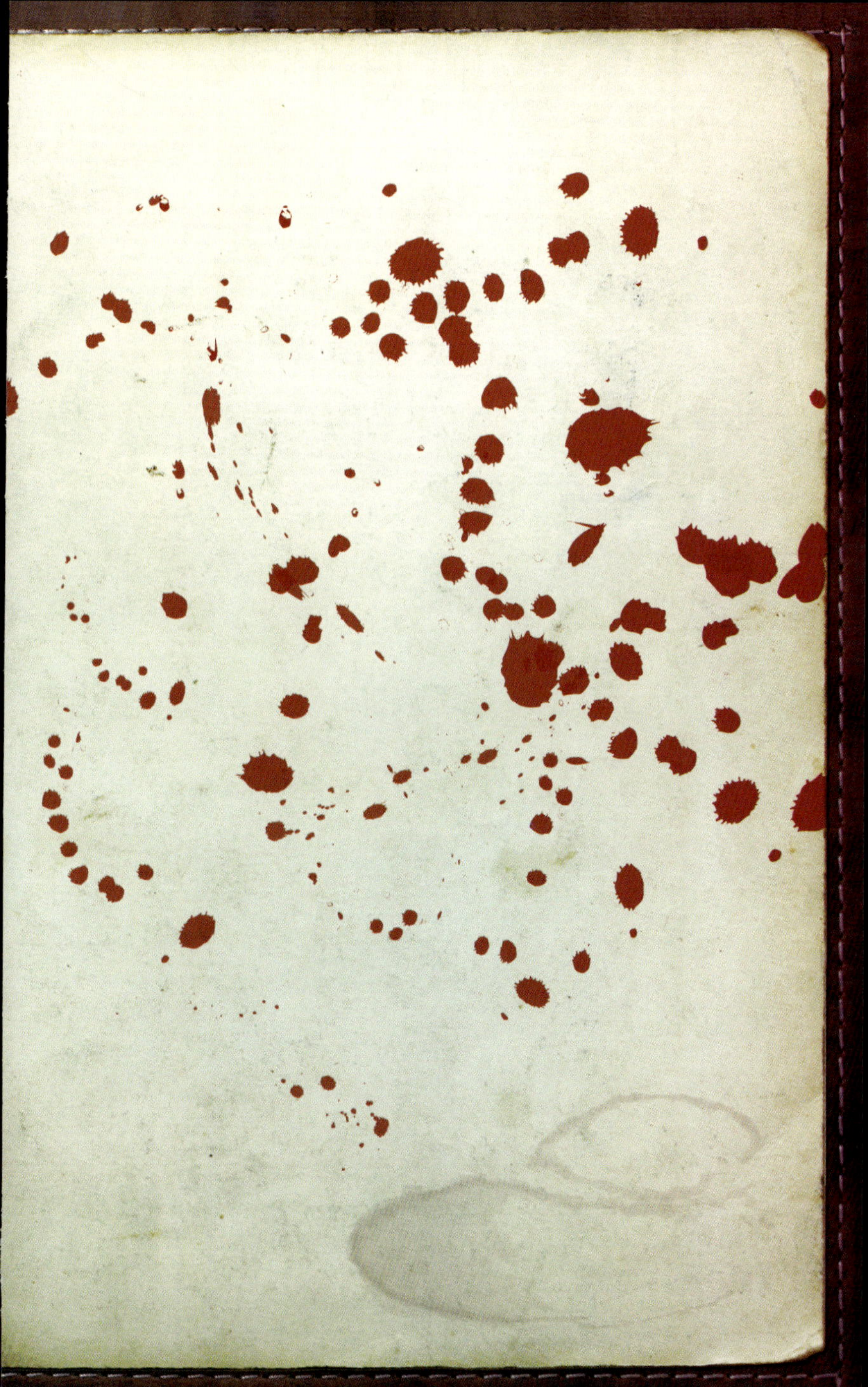

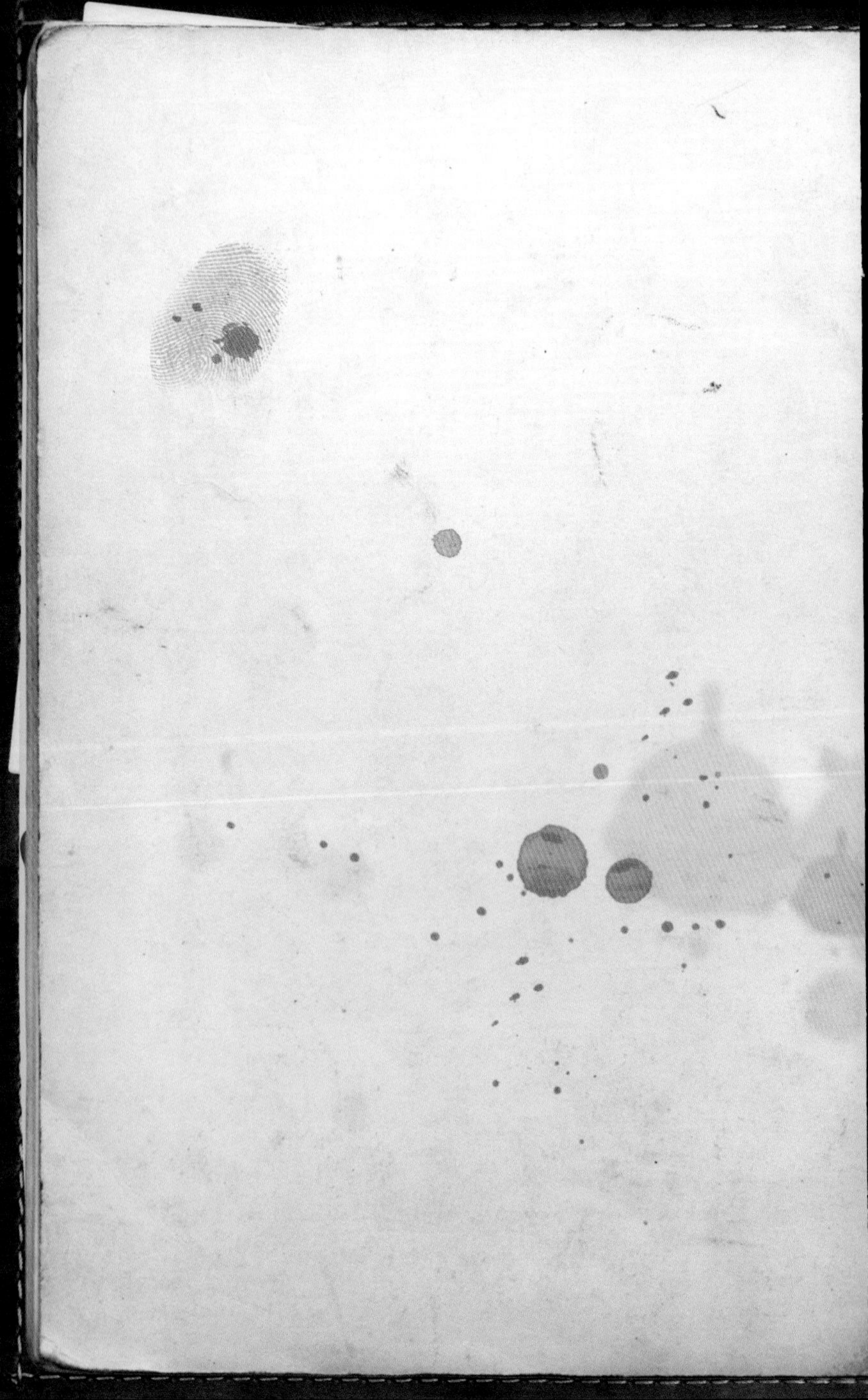